Cincinnati Art Museum Handbook

This project is supported by a grant from the
National Endowment for the Arts, a Federal agency in
Washington, D.C. Matching funds were provided
by a generous grant from The Thomas J. Emery Memorial.

Cincinnati Art Museum, Eden Park,
Cincinnati, Ohio 45202

Contents

Dedicated to
Director Emeritus Philip Rhys Adams
Director of the Cincinnati Art Museum
1945-1973

Introduction

Art museums have four basic purposes: to collect, to exhibit, to preserve and to interpret works of art. Since 1881, the Cincinnati Art Museum has been dedicated to these purposes, and this Handbook testifies to the accomplishments of a collecting, vital, growing institution. But the development of a great collection and its coverage of the history of art as recorded only through printed words and illustrations may seem, at best, impersonal and dry.

Admittedly, a primary ingredient lacking in a publication like this is the interaction between the art object itself and the visitor who experiences it. Certainly a museum's primary role is to create an environment in which the widest possible public is encouraged to share in the study and enjoyment of its art treasures. Hopefully, this publication suggests to this public some of the specific tools through which this interaction is possible.

Likewise, this Handbook indicates many of the generous individuals who have provided financial support through gifts and bequests for endowments and the many others who have donated to the Museum some of the art objects illustrated on the pages which follow. The benefactors' love for and interest in the Museum can only be implied, however, in this summary overview of the collection they have so enriched over the years. This publication may serve as partial testimony to the Museum's gratitude for their support. Where an object is listed simply as "Museum purchase" or "gift by subscription," it was acquired by combining funds or the gifts of a group of people too numerous to publish in a handbook of this size. Nevertheless, we are grateful for the contributions that made these purchases possible.

Whether or not this Handbook accompanies the visitor through the galleries, or becomes a library reference for the scholar and student, it records highlights of this collection from its beginnings in 1881 through 1974. It supersedes guide books to the collection published in 1952 and 1956, both now out-of-print and much smaller in format and coverage. The Museum's curatorial staff selected the most important and interesting objects in their areas of concern, and the project was coordinated by Assistant Director Betty L. Zimmerman and edited by Registrar and Assistant General Curator Carolyn R. Shine. Under their skilled guidance and the talents of Designer Noel Martin, this complex project was completed.

A publication of this magnitude would not be possible without the generous support of the National Endowment for the Arts and The Thomas J. Emery Memorial (which was established by Mary M. Emery, his wife), who provided matching grants to the Cincinnati Art Museum for this project. Their assistance is deeply appreciated.

It is fitting that this Handbook, a splendid selection of treasures from one of our country's great art museums, is dedicated to Director Emeritus Philip R. Adams. It was he who directed this institution for twenty-eight of its most glorious years, from 1945 to 1973, a period when the most important objects illustrated herein were acquired.

Millard F. Rogers, Jr.
Director

History of the Museum

The Cincinnati Art Museum is the first general art museum west of the Alleghenies to be established in its own building and is the oldest of Cincinnati's major cultural institutions. Its history closely parallels that of a city noted for its dedication to educational, cultural and religious pursuits from the time of its founding in the late eighteenth century. By as early as 1812 an art school already was established in Cincinnati, and by 1818 the first combined natural history and art museum was founded by Dr. Daniel Drake, a distinguished pioneer, scholar and physician. A survey of 1850 indicates that in the first half-century of its existence Cincinnati already had been home to more than eighty painters and twenty sculptors, and by 1854 the members of the Ladies' Fine Arts Academy (later a casualty of the Civil War) had made strides toward establishing a serious art gallery and school.

By 1877, the Women's Art Museum Association was formed, a continuation of the committee responsible for the successful exhibition by Cincinnati's women art potters and craftswomen at the Women's Pavilion of the Centennial Exposition in Philadelphia the preceding year. Their goals were to provide art classes, acquire collections and offer temporary art exhibitions for the city. It was at the opening of their internationally publicized art exhibition in September, 1880,

that Mr. Charles West of Cincinnati offered his generous gift of $150,000 for the founding of a permanent art museum, provided that the community could match his gift within one year. Just one month later some $160,000 had been pledged, and by 1881 the Cincinnati Museum Association, with Joseph Longworth as its first President, was formed. The new men's Board inherited the records, financial assets and collections of the women's Association which then disbanded.

In 1882, the City of Cincinnati granted to the new Museum a tract of nineteen acres of land for its building in Eden Park, atop Mt. Adams, the highest of the city's hills, just north of the business district. Here was constructed in the Richardson Romanesque style the colossal "Art Palace of the West" which opened to world acclaim in May, 1886. By October, 1887, its companion institution, the Art Academy of Cincinnati, was in being to offer professional training in the fine arts. Over the decades, the Museum building has undergone considerable enlargement to keep pace with the growth of the collections: in 1907 came the Schmidlapp Wing whose exterior Greek portico now is the main entrance; the Ropes Wing opened in 1910 and now houses exhibition galleries; the Emery, Hanna and French Wings of 1928-30 enclose the handsomely landscaped Garden Court; the Alms Wing of 1937 houses administrative offices, library, auditorium and temporary exhibition galleries; the newest Adams-Emery Wing of 1962-65 provides an increase of almost fifty percent in gallery space.

During the long decades since its founding the Cincinnati Art Museum has been favored by an almost unparalleled continuity of Board of Trustee leadership, with only six Presidents: Joseph Longworth, M. E. Ingalls, Charles P. Taft, Charles J. Livingood, John J. Emery (named Board Chairman in 1967), and John W. Warrington. The continuity of its professional leadership has been equally notable in that only four men served as

Museum Directors through 1973, each adding his own scholarly traits and creative interests to the ongoing growth of the permanent collections and special exhibitions: Alfred T. Goshorn, J. H. Gest, Walter H. Siple and Philip R. Adams (now Director Emeritus). Millard F. Rogers, Jr. became the fifth Director on September 1, 1974.

Today, the Museum offers to its visitor an almost complete review of the world's major civilizations through visual arts dating from over 5,000 years ago up to the present. The permanent collections of paintings, sculpture, graphic arts, costumes, period rooms and decorative arts occupy 118 galleries, with additional space reserved exclusively for temporary exhibitions.

The Museum is a privately incorporated institution, with a Board of Trustees elected by the Shareholders of the Cincinnati Museum Association. Its chief support comes from endowment funds, membership dues, admission fees, annual allocations from Cincinnati Fine Arts Fund which is a yearly campaign for the support of Cincinnati's four oldest cultural institutions, and from the thousands of gifts and bequests of art objects and monies which, since its founding, have come from local, national and international patrons.

Betty L. Zimmerman
Assistant Director

For the benefit of visitors to the Museum who may find use for this Handbook as a guide to what to look for, it should be noted that the works of art are presented in the Handbook in the social and chronological context in which they were created, although their physical location in the Museum may be in widely separated galleries, since this cultural complex can be counted on to remain constant while gallery arrangements are subject to frequent changes. It should be noted further that most of the objects presented in the Handbook should be regarded as standing for a whole class of comparable objects of which the Museum has several or many examples.

This is particularly true of certain classes of objects such as prints, drawings and textiles that are adversely affected by prolonged exposure to light. Individual prints, drawings and textiles are exhibited for a relatively short time and then given a rest while other comparable examples take their place on exhibition.

Since this is intended quite literally as a hand book, not as an exhaustive catalogue, the vital statistics which accompany the photographs have been held to a bare minimum. Dimensions are given, height preceding width, unless otherwise specified, and provenance, published references and exhibition history have been omitted. And finally, with respect to the preparation of the Handbook, it seems fitting to acknowledge that the explanatory text that introduces each section was largely prepared by Mr. Adams, and to give thanks to Elizabeth Shaffer who volunteered her services for the final typing of the manuscript.

Carolyn R. Shine
Registrar and Assistant
General Curator

Head of a Nome God, possibly Hapi, God of the
Nile, early Dynasty XII, limestone, height 10
inches, The John J. Emery Fund, 1970.170.

Egyptian Art

Man always has been an artist. Long before languages developed into more than a series of one-syllable nouns man had recorded his hopes, his fears, his attitudes to the world around him in highly sophisticated paintings and carvings. And he went on doing so as he evolved from hunter to herdsman to gourd farmer. Then, most significantly, he made the change to cereal farmer. Farming, or the agricultural revolution, meant fixed settlements with permanent habitation which required architecture. Gradually he also developed pottery to take the place of basketry. Basic to all systematic planting and harvesting, a calendar came into being, with the writing needed to record it. So history began.

Nowhere better than in Egypt can the story of these changes be seen. The growth of formal religions from their beginnings in ritual magic and totemism also can be clearly traced, with one exceptional Egyptian fea-

ture. That was a conviction, almost an obsession with the idea of immortality which gave Egyptian art a quality of monumental serenity and a continuity — not a uniformity — perhaps never equalled elsewhere. Elaborate burial rites developed, and preparation for the after life in the form of portraits and tomb furnishings was almost the chief occupation of Egyptian artists and craftsmen.

Among the most productive periods of Egyptian art were Dynasties IV and V of the so-called Old Kingdom (about 2900 to 2200 B.C.), after the Nile Valley had been unified and the copper mines of the Sinai developed. The great pyramids of this early time were accompanied by a brilliant style of portrait and figure sculpture. Then came the Middle Kingdom of Dynasties XI and XII (about 2050 to 1685 B.C.) with an art of vivid human-scale portrait sculpture. The New Kingdom or Empire (1570 to 1150 B.C.) produced an art of imperial, monumental

splendor, especially in Dynasty XVIII which ended on the note of Ikhnaton's (Amenhotep IV's) delicate naturalism stressing the "truth" of things. Dynasty XIX revived and even exaggerated the monumental style, but after it a general economic, political and artistic decline set in when Egypt was conquered by Assyrians, Persians, and finally the Greeks under Alexander the Great. But stimulated by Greek contacts in the Delta, Dynasty XXVI (663 to 525 B.C.) consciously attempted to revive the classic past, as did the Ptolemaic, or Greek period of Dynasties XXXI to XXXIII (332 to 30 B.C.).

Christianity came to Egypt fairly early in the Roman period, and Coptic art (about 200 to 639 A.D.), as the style of Christian Egypt is called, took on a distinct personality, anticipating later Islamic art and strongly affecting the early Christian west.

Palette in the Shape of a Fish, pre-Dynastic period, 4000-3000 B.C., slate, height 2 17/32 inches, Museum purchase, 1962.700.

This ceremonial palette, possibly a symbol of the Nile, held ritual colors with which a priest or worshipper would paint his face to resemble a god or king, in a kind of sympathetic magic.

Tomb Relief from Saqqara, Dynasty V, 2750-2625 B.C., limestone with traces of paint, height 19 11/16 inches, gift of Junior League Docents on the tenth anniversary of their association with the Museum and the twenty-fifth anniversary of Philip R. Adams as Director, 1971.28.

Standing Figure of a Royal Scribe, inscribed with the name of Cenn-Beff-Ny, Chancellor of the Documents of the King, Dynasty XII, 2000-1788 B.C., black granite, height 18 inches, Museum purchase, 1945.62.

Lotus Cup, Dynasty XVIII, 1580-1350 B.C., glazed pottery, height 5 1/4 inches, given in honor of Mr. and Mrs. Charles F. Williams by their children, 1948.87.

Fragment of a Portrait of Queen Hatshepsut from Deir-el-Bahri, Dynasty XVIII, about 1493-1479 B. C., rose granite, height 10 1/2 inches, Museum purchase, 1945.63.

Hatshepsut was the first great woman of history. She was co-ruler of Egypt from 1501 to 1479 B. C. with her much younger close relative Thutmose III. Because she presumed to seize power and go through the coronation ritual of "rebirth" as a god, upon her death Thutmose systematically destroyed her portrait statues. This fragment remained after one blow of the hammer knocked off her crown, probably the White Crown of Upper Egypt, and another blow smashed the ceremonial beard whose chin-strap still can be seen.

Mummy Case of a General or Priest of Amen-hotep III, Dynasty XVIII, about 1411-1375 B. C., painted linen and gesso over wood frame, length inside 66 inches, gift of Millard F. and Edna F. Shelt, 1947.275.

Portrait of a Noblewoman with dedicatory inscription on the back, Dynasty XVIII, about 1385-1375 B. C., limestone with traces of paint, height 19 1/2 inches, given by his friends in memory of Joseph D. Nelson, Jr., 1966.266.

Lioness, Dynasty XVIII-XIX, 1580-1205 B. C., bronze with rock crystal eyes, height 5 1/2 inches, gift of Mr. and Mrs. John J. Emery, 1972.478.

Seti I Offering Truth to Thoth, Dynasty XIX, about 1313-1292 B. C., limestone with traces of paint, height 30 1/4 inches, Museum purchase, 1945.64.

This relief from his magnificent temple at Abydos depicts Seti I, titular founder and greatest ruler of Dynasty XIX, as he swears to the accuracy of his earthly records before the ibis-headed secretary of the gods, Thoth, by presenting the figure of Maat, god of judgment. The god, in turn, holds the *ankh* or symbol of life.

Bowl, Persian period, Dynasty XXVII, 525-404
B. C., "Mittrahaine" glazed pottery with mixed
Hellenistic and Near Eastern motifs, height
4 7/16 inches, Museum purchase, 1952.242.

Kneeling Horus, Dynasty XXVI-XXX, 663-322
B.C., bronze, height 10 11/16 inches, gift of
Mr. and Mrs. James H. Stone, 1957.145.
    The scored surface of this hawk god, pro-
tector of royalty, suggests that a thin layer of
gold originally was pressed over the figure, with
the eyes and other features like the striped head-
dress probably inlaid with colored glass.

Ptolemy Philadelphos Offers a Libation, fragment of incised relief with offertory inscriptions, from Sebennytos, 285-247 B. C., granite, height 52 1/4 inches, Museum purchase, 1952.8.

Ptolemy Philadelphos was the inheritor of Alexander the Great's conquest of Egypt and builder of the famous Pharos or Lighthouse of Alexandria, one of the Seven Wonders of the Ancient World. His title of Ptolemy descends from the name of Alexander's general who was the first Greek ruler of Egypt.

Vase, Ptolemaic Dynasty, I-II century A. D., glazed pottery with relief decoration, height 6 7/8 inches, given in honor of Mr. and Mrs. Charles F. Williams by their children, 1948.88.

Capital, Coptic, probably from Medinet-al-Fayum, V century A. D., limestone, height 20 1/2 inches, Museum purchase, 1952.9.

The basic Corinthian shape and acanthus leaves of this capital are Graeco-Roman in style, but the crisply undercut carving emphasizes a flat pattern of light and dark that is characteristically Coptic.

Niche-Head, Coptic, from Bawit, V-VI century A. D., limestone, height 20 7/8 inches, Museum purchase, 1953.123.

Female Figure, Cycladic, about 2500 B. C., said to have been found on the island of Iraklia, marble, height 26 3/16 inches, Museum purchase, 1960.484.

Figures like this one are pre-Hellenic and have been found only on the islands of the Cyclades in the Aegean Sea. They are found in graves in recumbent positions, but their purpose still is not clear. This unusually large example is one of the most ancient sculptures in the Museum.

Greek, Etruscan, Roman and Nabataean Art

The first art of the Greek world was the stylized, highly modern-looking sculpture produced as early as 2800 B. C. by an unknown people of the Cycladic Islands in the Aegean Sea. Then another people of unknown origin and language developed writing and created another strikingly decorative art in Crete from about 2300 to 1400 B. C. This travelled with the Cretan sea-borne commerce throughout the eastern Mediterranean. About 2000 B. C. the first true Greeks, speaking an Indo-European language, began to settle the mainland of Hellas, spreading to the coast of Asia Minor. Their arts, generally called Mycenaean from one of their chief cities, were bold, masculine variations of Cretan style.

After a long interim caused by the destructive wave of the Dorian invasion of about 1100 B. C., the last of the Greek migrations, geometric pottery decoration and Archaic Greek sculpture emerged, at first strongly influenced by Egypt. At about the same time the writing of the Greek epics began. Growing population and trade led the Greek city-states from about 800 to 600 B. C. to send out colonies, most fruitfully to southern Italy and Sicily, and Greek art began to affect the whole Mediterranean world. After the Persian wars of 490 to 479 B. C. the Archaic style with its marked appeal to modern taste began to soften into a more naturalistic phase, the era of Phidias, later of Praxiteles and Skopas and their many followers. Also red-figured pottery succeeded the more

Archaic black-figured vessels.

The Etruscans of central and northern Italy, whose language still is a mystery, were profoundly influenced by Greek art but rang their own highly individual variations on it. They collected Greek pottery and were themselves gifted ceramic artists and sculptors in bronze and terra-cotta.

The Etruscans were later absorbed by the Romans who began about 340 B. C. to unify the whole of Italy with their adaptable republican form of government, a political skill the Greeks singularly lacked. Later the Romans defeated Carthage and conquered Greece. Greek art and culture, however, conquered Rome, and in its Hellenistic phase, as distinguished from the earlier style called Hellenic, was carried by the expanding Roman Empire as far as Scotland in the west and to Mesopotamia in the east. This art was modified by the arts of Rome's conquered and neighboring peoples, especially in the Near East and Coptic Egypt.

On the fringes of the Arabian Desert, in Palmyra and in southern Palestine, striking modifications occurred. Examples can be seen in the Museum's unique collection of Nabataean sculptures from Khirbet Tannur. A Near Eastern feeling for bold pattern and stylized arabesque line sharpens, flattens and undercuts the opulent naturalistic shapes of Graeco-Roman style, preparing the way for the Christian art of the early Middle Ages.

Votive Mirror with Figure of Artemis, from the Peloponnesus, Greece, or from Ionian Asia Minor, early VI century B. C., bronze, height 14 13/16 inches, gift of Michael Schaible in honor of his father, 1955.791.

This archaic Greek mirror was not designed for boudoir use; it was a woman's prayer to Artemis, the sister of Apollo, to be placed in the treasury of the goddess's temple.

Kylix and Bowl from Zygouries, Greece, late Helladic III, about 1350 B. C., pottery, height 4 1/8 and 6 1/4 inches, The William T. and Louise Taft Semple Collection, 1962.734-735.

Amphora by the Swing Painter, Attic, about 540 B. C., slip-painted pottery, height 19 1/2 inches, Museum purchase, 1959.1.

Subjects of this amphora, which shows the black-figured style at its zenith, are Herakles and Busiris, the King of Egypt, whose custom it was to sacrifice as a charm against drought all strangers who came to his land. The Egyptians were about to sacrifice Herakles, but at the last minute he turned the tables on the King and his dismayed attendants.

Warrior, Etruscan, from north-central Italy, VI-V century B. C., bronze, height 10 7/16 inches, gift of William Baer, 1906.40.

This votive figure was intended as an offering· to the Etruscan God of War in the hope of success in battle.

Head of Hermes, Attic, late VI century B. C., marble with traces of color, height 6 5/16 inches, The William T. and Louise Taft Semple Collection, 1962.390.

The shoulders of this bearded male head, characteristic of the early Greek style called Archaic, are shaped into the dressed sides of a "herm" or boundary marker. It is said to have been found at Vrona near Markopoulo, Attica.

Doe's Head Finials, from the region of Sybaris, South Italy, about 400 B. C., gold over bronze, height 7 1/2 inches, Museum purchase, 1957.467-468.

These finials may have been used as crests rising from the back of a chair or couch. Their decorative richness suggests their origin in Sybaris, the Achaean Greek colony on the Gulf of Tarentum, whose name has become the synonym for extravagant luxury.

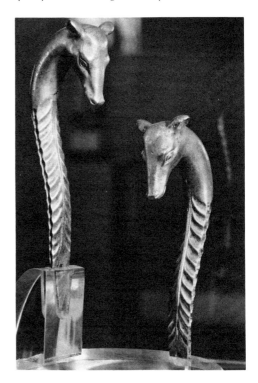

Head of a Woman, Attic, late IV century B. C.,
marble, height 8 7/8 inches, The William T. and
Louise Taft Semple Collection, 1962.389.

Loutrophoros, Attic, IV century B. C., marble
with traces of color, height 53 1/4 inches, The
William T. and Louise Taft Semple Collection,
1962.416.

The shape of this marble grave marker is
taken from the pottery vessel called a loutrophoros from which the bridal bath was poured.
Greeks from the earliest times placed pottery
vessels both in the grave and on it to hold liba-
tions for the gods of the Underworld. The loutrophoros was used only for the graves of the un-
married, symbolically providing them in death
with the wedding ceremony they had missed in
life.

Lion, Attic, late IV century B. C., Pentelic marble, height 33 1/4 inches, Museum purchase, 1946.40.

This was a funerary monument, possibly for the grave of a military leader.

Bull, probably Attic, bronze, height 12 5/16 inches, The John J. Emery Fund, 1956.13.

This commanding bronze may have been intended as a symbol of Zeus, whose special animal was the bull and who sometimes took the form of a bull. Its date is still uncertain, some scholars dating it to the late Archaic VI century B. C., and others as late as the Hellenistic period.

Asklepios, Attic, early III century B. C., bronze, height 9 3/8 inches, gift of Michael Schaible in honor of his father, 1957.504.

This work in the full classic style, suggesting the art of Skopas, depicts the Greek god of medicine, son of Apollo and the mortal maiden Coronis. His powers of healing were inherited from his father and were so great that he could bring the dead back to life. His hand may have held a scroll or a *caduceus,* a winged staff with serpents which is the symbol of medicine.

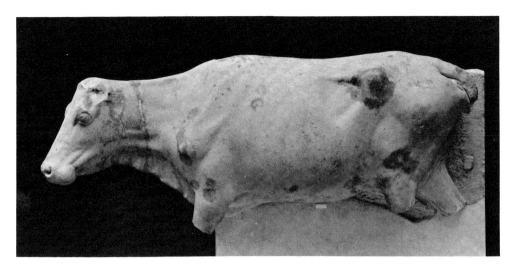

Heifer, Attic, III century B. C., Parian marble, height 19 7/8 inches, The John J. Emery Fund, 1946.9.

Cattle were impressive offerings to the gods throughout Greek history. The sculptor Myron, active from 480 to 445 B. C., fashioned a life-size bronze sacrificial heifer which stood on the Acropolis in Athens for several centuries, and then disappeared. This marble is a copy by a Greek sculptor of the third century B. C.

Head of a Faun, probably from Western Asia Minor, III-I century B. C., marble, height 9 5/8 inches, gift of Mr. and Mrs. John J. Emery, 1966.5.

Portrait Head of a Man, Roman, Republican period, II-I century B. C., marble, height 18 inches, gift of William H. Chatfield, 1957.485.

Portrait Head of a Woman, possibly Julia Domna,
wife of the Emperor Septimius Severus, Roman,
about 195 A. D., Italian marble, height 9 13/16
inches, Museum purchase, 1946.5.

Sacred Relief: Mithras Sacrificing the Bull, from
the Via Praeneste, Rome, late II century A. D.,
limestone, height 24 5/8 inches, gift of Mr. and
Mrs. Fletcher E. Nyce, 1968.112.

Mithraism is a later aspect of the ancient
Persian religion, Zoroastrianism, which con-
ceived of the universe in endess confict between
good as personified by the god Ahuramazda
whose symbol is the sun, and Ahriman, the force
of evil and darkness. About the third century
B. C., Mithras, an earlier messenger or "messiah,"
emerged as Ahuramazda's divine mediator between mortals and the abstract nature of the
absolute god. By the second century A.D.
Mithraism had swept even to the western Roman
empire as the almost exclusive religion of the
Legions. A sacred relief like this one was as
essential to a Mithraic shrine as relics of a saint
or the Host itself to a Roman Catholic altar.

Head of an East Roman Emperor, Byzantine, first
half of V century A. D., marble, height 14 1/16
inches, Museum purchase, 1973.292.

Cup, from Tyre, Roman period, I century B. C.-
I century A. D., glazed pottery, height 3 1/8
inches, Museum purchase, 1952.243.

Tomb Portrait of Malocha, Son of Nur-Bel, from
Palmyra, Syria, II century A. D., limestone with
traces of color, incised Aramaic inscription,
height 20 3/4 inches, gift of E. S. David, 1958.257.

Bust of Tyche Crowned with the Zodiac, from
Khirbet Tannur, Nabataea (Jordan), I-II century
A. D., limestone, height 11 5/8 inches, gift by
subscription, 1939.233.

Cult Figure of Zeus-Hadad in front of the **East Facade of the Period II Altar-Base**, from Khirbet Tannur, Nabataea (Jordan): the Altar-Base, limestone, about 8-7 B. C., height 112 inches; Zeus-Hadad, sandstone, height 45 1/16 inches; gift by subscription, 1939.223-224.

Zeus-Hadad, the chief god of the Nabataeans, is shown here in a Greek-derived costume, wearing chiton, himation and lion-headed neck torque. The thunderbolt in his left hand and probably a sceptre in his right hand (broken off), along with the kneeling bulls at his feet, are symbols of his power.

Kneeling Hero Bound with Serpents, Sumerian, from Tello (ancient Lagash), about 2800 B. C., alabaster, height 11 13/16 inches, The Mary Hanna Fund, 1957.33.

The subject of this figure has not yet been interpreted; it has a heroic bearing yet is captive. It could be the hero Gilgamesh, the prototype of Hercules, shown as a captive of evil. The fish hanging from his neck may represent the Tigris and Euphrates, or be the symbols of a river god or possibly one of the city-states.

Votive Calf, Sumerian, from Mesopotamia, about 2300 B. C., bronze, height 11 1/4 inches plus overhang of tail, The Mary Hanna Fund, 1957.32.

This engaging animal, whose tail is socketed to swing, has full-grown horns to show that he is unmistakably a bull, yet is depicted as a calf so newly born that his skin is wrinkled on his legs and head. He is a visible prayer offered to an ancient god of fertility.

Near Eastern Art: Ancient and Islamic

As Mesopotamia, the marshy valley between the Euphrates and Tigris Rivers, began to dry out, Semitic-speaking peoples from Arabia settled Akkad in the northern part. Another people who spoke a non-Semitic language came in from the east to settle Sumer in the south. These Sumerians, whose First Dynasty of Ur dates from about 3000 B. C., developed a system of writing called "cuneiform" from its wedge-shaped marks on clay tablets, along with commercial, legal, agricultural, and astronomical practices still used today. Their original political organization was composed of city-states, some of which were strong enough to dominate others and hence were known as "kingly cities."

Since Mesopotamia had almost no timber or stone for building and sculpture, its early arts are small in size although sophisticated in style. By about 1800 B. C. the royal city of Babylon was so powerful that it ruled the whole valley, partly by means of the famous legal code named for its greatest king, Hammurabi.

While Babylonia produced few works of art that have survived, the Assyrians to the north as early as 1116 B. C. were developing a monumental art to match the martial character of the empire they were building. Their sculpture was carved from large blocks and slabs of alabaster and other stone rafted down from the mountains of Asia Minor where they also got the iron that gave them military superiority over the bronze weapons

of their subject peoples. The Assyrians also worked gold, bronze, ivory and rock crystal with unsurpassed skill. When the Assyrian capital Nineveh fell to allied Babylonians and Medes in 612, Babylon flourished again until it was taken by Cyrus the Persian in 538 B. C.

The Medes and Persians, who spoke the Aryan branch of the Indo-European language family, came onto the high Iranian plateau from central Asia sometime between 2000 and 1500 B. C. Contact by trade and war with the Mesopotamian powers stimulated the first Persian arts, the bronze and silver horse-trappings and talismans from Luristan in the Zagros mountains dating from about 1100 to 800 B. C. These already show the symbols of the dualistic religion characteristic of Persian thought. Then in the Median north the Amlash culture and the Mannaean masterpieces of Ziwiye further developed the style.

In 550 B. C. Cyrus began to unite the Medes with their blood brothers the Persians to found one of the greatest empires of antiquity. Darius (521 to 485 B. C.) and his successor Xerxes built the superb palace-shrine of Persepolis whose primarily native Persian sculpture style in stone, silver and gold was influenced by Greek and Egyptian art. This Achaemenid period, named for its ruling dynasty, ended with Alexander's conquest in 330 B. C. and the brief rule of his Seleucid generals and their descendants.

Then the Arsacid Dynasty of the Parthians,

native Persians, ruled for a little over four hundred years, leaving behind distinguished arts only recently rediscovered. The Sasanian Dynasty came next, from 227 to 642 A. D., with an art noted for its brilliant silk weaving and metal work as well as for truly monumental sculpture. Sasanian arts had a profound effect on the arts of the East Christian world with which it was in constant touch.

Sasanian culture did not die with the Islamic conquest in the seventh century. The Persian Abbasid Caliphate that ruled Islam from 750 to about 1100 in Baghdad paid little heed to the Prophet Mohammed's prohibition of graven images, making use of floral, animal and human shapes in weaving, painting, pottery and sculpture.

Then the Seljuk Dynasty, whose rulers were originally Turkish, brought Persian Islamic arts to a climax of great pottery and manuscript illumination in the twelfth and early thirteenth centuries. The Mongol conquest introduced the Il-Khan Dynasty which quickly became more Persian than the Persians, as did the Timurid Dynasty of Tamerlane and his successors. At last the Safavid Dynasty (1500-1736) with its most famous patron of the arts, Shah Abbas (1587-1629), brought architecture, weaving and manuscript illumination to their absolute heights.

The arts of Islamic India, Turkey, Syria, Egypt and Moorish Spain parallel these Persian accomplishments and often derive from them. Turkey and Moorish Spain are especially noted for their pottery and weaving.

Horned Animal, from Anatolia, second half of third millenium B. C., bronze, height 2 15/16 inches, given in memory of William Harry Gothard by his friends, 1969.86.

Portrait Head, from the province of Azerbaijan, Persia, about 1800 B. C., bronze, height 5 7/8 inches, Museum purchase, 1958.520.

Breast Plaque or Belt Appliqué, from the region of Luristan, Persia, 1100-800 B. C., silver, height 4 5/8 inches, Museum purchase, 1957.29.

This silver plaque, probably worn on the chest of a priest-king, represents one of the most complex religious statements in early Persian civilization. It suggests the twin birth of the gods represented by the constellation Gemini, or possibly Ahuramazda, god of the sun and cosmic force of good, and Ahriman, god of darkness and evil, parallels to the Greek demigods Castor and Pollux, or their prototypes.

Cheekplates and Bit, from the region of Luristan, Persia, 1100-800 B. C., bronze, height 7 7/8 inches. Museum purchase, 1958.542.

Ceremonial Cauldron, from the region of Luristan, Persia, 1100-800 B. C., bronze, height including handle 12 1/8 inches, The Mary Hanna Fund, 1957.225.

Priest in Ritual Costume, from Calah, Assyria, 883-859 B. C., alabaster, height 36 inches, Museum purchase, 1952.7.

Head of a Bull, Urartian, from the region of Lake Van, IX-VIII century B. C., bronze, height 5 31/32 inches, gift of John J. Emery, 1973.679.

Pectoral, Mannaean, from the Treasure of Ziwiye,
Kurdistan region of Persia, IX-VIII century B. C.,
gold, height 8 3/8 inches, The Mary Hanna and
John J. Emery Funds, 1953.67, 1963.402.

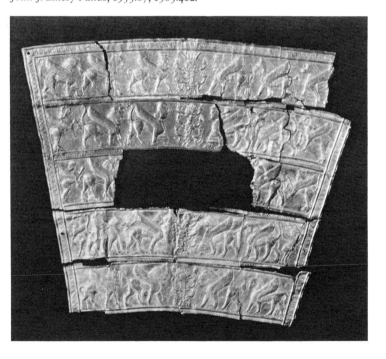

Assyrian Priest, said to be from the Treasure of
Ziwiye, Kurdistan region of Persia, 725-700 B. C.,
ivory, height 7 15/16 inches, gift of Mr. and Mrs.
Warner L. Atkins, 1955.70.

Bowl with Relief of Lions Hunting Bulls, Assyrian, VIII-VII century B. C., rock crystal, height 3 1/4 inches, Museum purchase, 1957.500.

This royal cup, the largest and most elaborately decorated rock crystal vessel yet known in ancient Near Eastern art, is said to have been found in the Persian capital, Persepolis, possibly carried there as booty from Nineveh or Babylon. Considering the difficulties of working rock crystal, this depiction of lions stalking and killing a bull, with the male chasing his prey into the jaws of the lioness, is rendered with startling intensity.

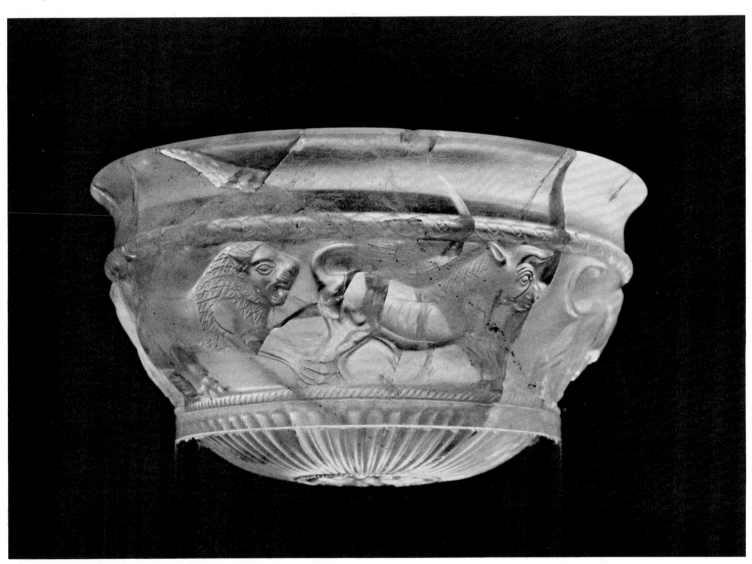

Beaker, Amlash culture, Persia, VIII-VII century B. C., gold, height 8 1/4 inches, Museum purchase, 1962.71.

Cup with Ibex Handles, Median, from Hamadan, Persia, VI-V century B. C., gold, height to top of handles 4 1/2 inches, gift of Mr. and Mrs. John J. Emery, 1956.82.

Such was the Persians' intimate knowledge of animals that here the double heads of the ibex suggest that even while drinking he is alert and looks around for possible enemies.

Rhyton with Kneeling Bull, Persian, Achaemenid Dynasty, VI-V century B. C., silver, height 8 1/2 inches, Museum purchase, 1958.519.

This *rhyton,* or drinking vessel with a base to hold it upright, takes its shape from the bull's horn used for very ancient cups. Its base is the kneeling bull, a symbol of royalty very similar to the bulls on the capitals that rise from the columns at Susa and Persepolis.

Libation Dish of Darius the Great, Persian, from Hamadan, 522-485 B. C., gold, diameter 12 inches, Museum purchase, 1963.31.

This royal wine dish bears the name of Darius the Great, "King of Kings," incised on the back in the cuneiform characters of the Old Persian, Elamite and Neo-Babylonian or Akkadian languages. Such a splendid vessel was for ceremonial use, probably for great state occasions or religious festivals.

Attendant Carrying a Wineskin, relief from Persepolis, Persia, probably early Reign of Xerxes, about 484-482 B. C., limestone, height 22 5/8 inches, Museum purchase, 1951.133.

Darius the Great began construction of Persepolis, his ceremonial capital, about 518-516 B. C., and it still was unfinished when Alexander the Great burned it in 330 B. C. The Achaemenid court was in residence there only for the short time of the vernal equinox, or New Year's festival, when tribute poured in from the far reaches of the empire. This relief of a full-trousered and beardless noble Median page who steps upward to carry his wineskin to the private royal quarters, comes from the outside parapet of the south stairway of the Tachari, residence quarters of Darius.

Armlet, Persian, from Hamadan, Achaemenid Dynasty, VI-IV century B. C., gold with terminals of lapis lazuli paste, diameter 4 7/8 inches, The John J. Emery Fund, 1957.30.

Feudal service to the king, as in later medieval Europe, was a duty and a privilege of the Persian aristocrat, performed at his own expense. If such service was too costly for some, a royal gift like this armlet could compensate. It also was a military decoration for exceptional valor.

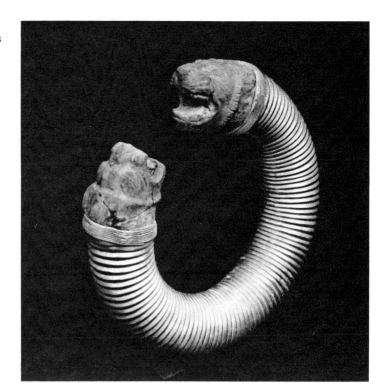

Ewer, Parthian, from Persia or Eastern Roman Empire, I century A. D., bronze, height 8 5/8 inches, Museum purchase, 1967.469.

Ewer, Persian, Sasanian Dynasty, IV-V century A. D., silver, height 16 1/8 inches, The Mary Hanna and John J. Emery Funds, 1966.1091.

Wine Dish with Duck Rondels, Persian, from the province of Mazanderan, Sasanian Dynasty, V century A. D., silver, diameter 11 7/16 inches, Museum purchase, 1951.131.

This shallow plate or wine dish is typical of the luxurious trappings of Sasanian nobility. It depicts the *hamsa* or waterfowl, a potent symbol of power because it inhabits the three elements of earth, air and water.

Plate, Persian, IX-X century A. D., glazed pottery, diameter 13 5/8 inches, given in honor of Mr. and Mrs. Charles F. Williams by their children, 1948.93.

Capital, Hispano-Moresque, from the region of Cordoba, Spain, X century A. D., marble, height 9 5/16 inches, given in memory of Louise O. and Arthur L. Zimmerman by their children, 1971.29.

Bottle, from Rayy, Persia, late XII century A. D., pottery with lustre glaze, height 10 1/4 inches, Museum purchase, 1952.255.

Polo Game, illustration from the *Andarz Name*, color on paper, 14 3/8 by 8 1/8 inches, gift of Audrey Emery, 1954.412.

The *Andarz Name* or *Book of Counsel*, composed in 1082 A. D. by Kayus ibn Iskandar ibn Kapus ibn Vusmgir, became a classic of Persian literature, and many copies were written and illustrated by hand long before printing existed. This page comes from a manuscript from Gurgan, Persia, signed by Sirda ibn Sirdid al-Isfahbadi at-Tabari and dated 1090 A. D., of which the Museum owns approximately half, the other half being in a private collection.

Storage Jar, from Sultanabad, Persia, XIII century
A. D., glazed pottery, height 28 inches, given in
honor of Mr. and Mrs. Charles F. Williams by
their children, 1948.100.

Plate, from Rakka, Syria, XII century A. D.,
glazed pottery, diameter 14 inches, given in
honor of Mr. and Mrs. Charles F. Williams by
their children, 1948.116.

Bowl, from Rayy, Persia, XII-XIII century A. D.,
glazed and enameled pottery, height 6 9/16
inches, given in honor of Mr. and Mrs. Charles
F. Williams by their children, 1948.108.

Lion, probably from Sava, Persia, Seljuk Dynasty,
XIII century A. D., glazed pottery, height
23 13/32 inches, Museum purchase, 1958.518

Moses Strikes the Giant Uj, illustration from a
manuscript of the *Majma al-tawarikh* by Hafiz-I
Abru, from Herat, Persia, about 1425 A. D., color
on paper, 16 3/4 by 12 7/8 inches, Museum
purchase, 1947.501.

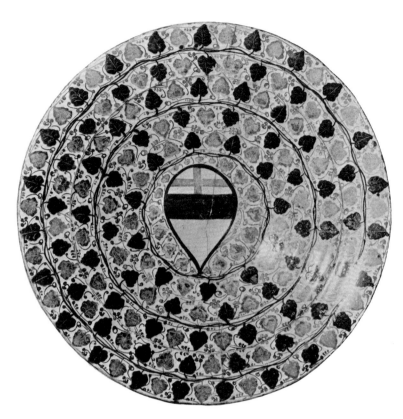

Hispano-Moresque Plate, from Valencia, Spain,
XV century A. D., glazed pottery, diameter
17 1/4 inches, given in honor of Mr. and Mrs.
Charles F. Williams by their children, 1948.131.

Hispano-Moresque Carpet, from Alcaraz, Spain,
XV-XVI century A. D., knotted wool pile, 244
by 113 inches, gift of Mr. and Mrs. John J.
Emery, 1966.638.

Plate, from Damascus, Syria, XVI century A. D., glazed pottery, diameter 14 1/2 inches, given in honor of Mr. and Mrs. Charles F. Williams by their children, 1948.135.

Young Man Playing a Lute, School of Tabriz, Persia, first half of XVI century A. D., color on paper, 13 5/8 by 9 1/4 inches, gift of John W. Warrington, 1948.190.

Mug, from Isnik, Turkey, XVI century A. D., glazed pottery, height 8 1/4 inches, given in honor of Mr. and Mrs. Charles F. Williams by their children, 1948.140.

Tomb Cover, from the Shrine of the Imam Riza in Meshed, Persia, late XVI-early XVII century A. D., knotted silk pile incorporating a dedicatory poem and the signature of Muhammed Ja'far Kashani, 120 by 42 inches, Museum purchase, 1953.124.

The Imam Riza was the foremost Persian martyr saint, killed by a nephew of Harun al-Rashid in the eleventh century. His tomb at Meshed became the principal pilgrimage shrine of eastern Islam, and this tomb cover was one of its choicest treasures. The inscription dedicates it to Shah Abbas, thus dating it in his reign, 1589-1627. Its central panel shows a "Paradise Garden," with a pool, trees flowering and bearing autumn leaves all at once, and the phoenix and the *hamsa,* or waterfowl, above. In the border is shown the oracular *waq-waq* tree with the four archangels of the Moslem paradise.

Prayer Cloth of Shah Abbas, from Isfahan, Persia, about 1620 A. D., silk and silver compound weave incorporating the inscription, "There is no God but God, and He is one, and He has no partner," 49 by 33 inches, gift of Mr. and Mrs. John J. Emery, 1966.1180.

Garden Carpet, from northwest Persia, late XVI or early XVII century A. D., knotted wool pile, 168 by 74 inches, gift of Mr. and Mrs. John J. Emery, 1966.1181.

Dish from Kütahya, Turkey, attributed to the Armenian potter "Chorister T'oros (Theodoros)," glazed pottery, diameter 5 7/8 inches, Museum purchase, 1952.271.

The Armenian inscription over the figure's head identifies him as St. Sargis (Sergius), and below the horse is the Armenian date 1168 (A. D. 1718). On the back is the monogram of Abraham Vardapet for whom the dish was made.

Mihrab, Persian, XVII-XVIII century A. D., glazed pottery mosaic. height 106 1/2 inches, gift of The Museum Shop Committee and Volunteers, 1971.59.

Islamic places of worship are oriented toward the Holy City, Mecca, with the wall of the mosque facing Mecca marked by a niche called the *mihrab*. The tiles of this *mihrab* are glazed in blue and green, perhaps the most esteemed colors in the Islamic world, and the border is formed by an inscription from the Koran.

Room from a House in Damascus, Syrian, XVIII century A. D., carved, painted and inlaid wood, gift of Andrew Jergens, 1966.443.

Indian and Southeast Asian Art

An Aryan-speaking people moved into India from central Asia sometime between 2000 and 1200 B. C., dominating the aboriginal population and developing a caste system to reinforce their control. They also developed the first great Indian religion, based on a trinity of gods with various *avatars,* or earthly manifestations.

But another great religion, Buddhism, named for its founder, "the enlightened one," who lived from about 563 to 483 B. C., stimulated the first important arts of India. At almost the same time Jainism, another religious philosophy, also took form with its distinctive arts. Asoka, a ruler of the Maurya Dynasty (321 to 184 B. C.), spread Buddhism throughout the whole subcontinent and into Ceylon. Tradition says that he raised 80,000 stupas, or temple mounds, over relics of the Buddha. They were richly carved with symbolic representations of the Buddha and detailed depictions of his life.

In the Indus Valley to the north, especially in the region of Gandhara, Hellenistic influence from the west gave the Buddha and his *Bodhisattvas,* or apostles, human form. Such sculptures were the missionaries of Buddhism as it travelled to China, Burma, Malaya and Cambodia, Siam, Japan, and even as far as the island of Java. By the seventh century A. D., however, Buddhism yielded to a revival of the earlier religions in its homeland, while flourishing in Nepal as well as southeastern Asia. The eighth and ninth centuries produced a brilliant art in Java, as did the tenth to thirteenth centuries in Cambodia.

Islam was firmly established in northern India by the tenth century A. D., but reached its artistic climax during the Mughal, or Mogul Dynasty (1526 to 1761). Persian in artistic inspiration, the Mughals developed architecture, weaving and miniature painting that rival the masterpieces of Persia. A certain tropical luxuriance, however, distinguishes them from the purity and austerity of their models.

India

Buddhist Relief, from the region of Amaravati, South India, Andhra Dynasty, late II-early III century A. D., marble with traces of sizing and red paint, height 20 19/32 inches, anonymous gift, 1952.187.

This marble relief depicting the Buddha and his Princely Companions comes from the classical culmination of Indian Buddhist art which flowered in what is now the province of Madras. Here the Buddha's footprints on a footstool most actively suggest his human presence, while on the empty throne a circular cushion with a curving swastika may symbolize his universal presence.

Seated Buddha, from Swat, region of Gandhara, North India, II-III century A. D., gray schist, height 26 7/8 inches, The William T. and Louise Taft Semple Collection, 1962.455.

Siva Nataraja, from the region of Madras, India, XVI-XVII century A. D., bronze, height 33 13/16 inches, gift of George Warrington in memory of Elsie Holmes Warrington, 1940.1079.

The trinity of the ancient Aryans who invaded and dominated India about 2000 B. C. is made up of Brahma, god of gods, the universe itself; Vishnu, who by his divine sleep strengthens and rejuvenates the universe; Siva, the force of life as both preserver and destroyer. When Siva wakes and dances, the world lives; when he tires and rests, it is destroyed by the sacred fire he holds in his upper left hand. His lower left hand makes the gesture of reassurance; his lower right holds the serpent of evil which he has overcome. He dances on the back of the dwarf Muyalaka, a spirit of evil, while the drum representing the sound and rhythm of life is held in his upper right hand and sets the tempo of his dance.

Badi Emerging from a Chest, illustration from a manuscript of the *Dastan-i-Amir Hamza,* by the Mughal imperial workshop, Delhi, India, early Reign of Akbar, about 1555-1570 A. D., color and gold leaf on cotton textile, 28 3/4 by 22 inches, gift of John W. Warrington, 1948.192.

Religious Mendicants at a Garden Pavilion, illustration from a Mughal manuscript, inscribed "Dharm Das," India, Reign of Akbar, 1556-1605 A. D., color on paper, 11 5/8 by 7 1/8 inches, gift of John J. Emery, 1950.288.

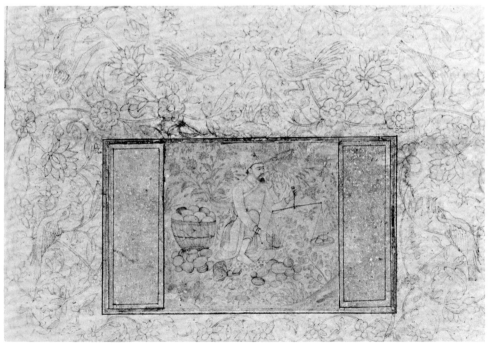

Man Weighing Vegetables, illustration from an album of the Mughal emperor Jahangir, India, about 1609-1613 A. D., ink and color on paper, 6 3/8 by 9 7/8 inches, gift of John J. Emery, 1949.151.

Jain Shrine, from Patan, Gujarat, India, XVII century A. D., wood carved, painted and gilded, height 85 3/8 inches, The William T. and Louise Taft Semple Collection, 1962.459.

Jainism was founded by the sage Mahavira, 599 to 527 B. C., a contemporary of the Buddha, and survives to this day. Its goal was the attainment of salvation through rebirth. Mahavira and his followers taught that salvation could be achieved through the practice of asceticism and through the scrupulous avoidance of injuring or killing a living creature.

Ceremonial Floorcloth (detail), from Golconda, Southeast India, XVII century A. D., dye-painted cotton textile, 272 by 182 inches, The William T. and Louise Taft Semple Collection, 1962.486.

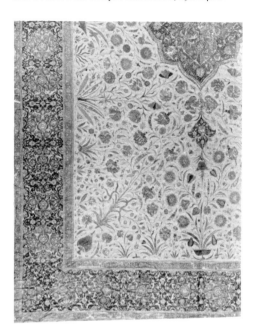

Shawl, from North India, XIX century A. D., cashmere wool, twill weave, 126 by 54 inches, gift of Mrs. Joseph Swan Neave and Ruth Harrison, 1934.48.

Southeast Asia

Head of A Dhyani Buddha, from Borobudur,
Java, VIII-IX century A. D., stone, height 13 1/8
inches, Museum purchase, 1952.113.

Avalokitesvara, from Nepal, XIV century A. D.,
bronze, height 24 3/4 inches, The William T. and
Louise Taft Semple Collection, 1962.445.

Female Bust, from Cambodia, about XIII century
A. D., gray sandstone, height 18 5/32 inches, The
William T. and Louise Taft Semple Collection,
1962.456.

Far Eastern Art

The oldest Chinese potteries are very like those of peoples in other parts of the world who were undergoing the agricultural revolution. But in the Shang Dynasty (1766 to 1122 B. C.) and succeeding Chou Dynasty (1122 to 255 B. C.) formal Chinese art suddenly flowered into magnificent bronze ritual vessels, perfect expressions of the patriarchal society of the period. Sacrifices to the gods of earth and sky and to the spirits of ancestors were prepared and offered in them. Metal-working may have been introduced to the Yellow River Valley from the Near East, since few experimental beginnings of such superb metallurgical skills have survived.

Chinese culture was fully matured by the time of Confucius (551 to 479 B. C.). The Han Dynasty (206 B. C. to 220 A. D.) brought imperial unity to the whole realm, and was in commercial and diplomatic touch with Rome which it parallels in time. The social code of Confucius and the Animism of his contemporary Lao-tzu were the chief religious forces in China until

Jar, Chinese, Neolithic, from Pan-shan region, about 2000 B. C., slip-painted pottery, height 11 1/4 inches, Museum purchase, 1950.41.

China

Fang-I (Ceremonial Vessel), Chinese, Shang Dynasty, 1766-1122 B. C., bronze, height with lid 11 3/8 inches, a single-character inscription impressed inside lid and inside bottom of vessel, given in honor of Mr. and Mrs. Charles F. Williams by their children, 1948.75.

Earliest of the great Chinese arts are the ritual bronzes of patriarchal China. The majority of

them were the prized possessions of royal and noble households. It is supposed that they held offerings of water and wine, raw and cooked meats and grains to be offered to the spirits of ancestors and the gods of heaven and earth. The shape of the bronze *fang-I,* like an actual Chinese granary with openings at the base, suggests that it held sacrificial grain.

Buddhism, newly arrived from India by way of the central Asian silk routes, was officially adopted by the Northern Wei Dynasty (386 to 534 A. D.). Its spiritual strength and nobility inspired some of the greatest of all monumental sculpture.

The Northern Ch'i Dynasty (565 to 575 A. D.) and the following Sui Dynasty (598 to 618 A. D.) were especially productive, as was the early phase of the powerful T'ang Dynasty (618 to 907 A. D.) with its strong trade and political ties to the Near East. Painting and pottery developed brilliantly in the T'ang Dynasty, tending to supplant sculpture, and reached classic perfection in the Sung Dynasty (960 to 1279 A. D.).

The Mongol Yüan Dynasty (1260 to 1368 A. D.), made known to Europe through Marco Polo's famous travels, continued the Sung tradition. The following Ming Dynasty (1368 to 1644 A. D.) cultivated all the arts, including the fine weaving for which China was always distinguished. The Ch'ing Dynasty (1644 to 1912) was largely content with variations on the great past, and through its sea-borne trade in textiles and tableware introduced Chinese craft skills as well as artistic modes to the Western world.

The long, relatively uninterrupted continuity of Chinese culture gives a superficial impression of uniformity to its arts, as is the case with Egypt. But closer acquaintance reveals as great a variety and individual vitality of style as can be found in the sculpture, paintings, pottery and other fine crafts of any people—and not many were as gifted.

The same is true of Japanese art. Japanese admiration for the older accomplishments of China led to emulation and sometimes outright imitation. However, no people as creative as the Japanese could conceal their vigorous individuality for long, and their sculpture and painting, as well as their superb pottery, textiles and lacquers, by no means are mere echoes of China. In the late nineteenth century the distinctive Japanese art of woodblock prints had almost as profound an effect on Western taste as Chinese art had exerted in the eighteenth century.

Chung (Bell), Chinese, late Chou Dynasty, 1122-255 B. C., bronze, height 16 11/16 inches, given in honor of Mr. and Mrs. Charles F. Williams by their children, 1948.76.

Kuang (Ceremonial Wine Pitcher), Chinese, Shang Dynasty, 1766-1122 B. C., bronze, height with lid 9 1/4 inches, given in honor of Mr. and Mrs. Charles F. Williams by their children, 1948.78.

Votive Stela with Buddhist Trinity, with dedicatory inscriptions on the back, Chinese, Wei Dynasty, 522 A. D., limestone, height 79 1/2 inches, The John J. Emery Fund, 1946.11.

When Buddhism was established in China by the Wei Dynasty, votive and memorial stelae sprang up overnight through the northern provinces. This stela is one of the earliest of them and it bears an inscription with the equivalent of the date 522 A. D. The subject, cut in relief, is a typical one: Buddha as the historic teacher, flanked by *Bodhisattvas,* saintly personages who have achieved nirvana but have chosen to remain in the world to help mankind. With his right hand the Buddha makes the gesture of assurance, and his left hand is in the position of charity. A pointed aureole flickering with engraved flames along its edges shapes the stone. A smaller aureole surrounds the Buddha's head with the Seven *Manushi,* or previous Buddhas. Around and above these, the *apsaras,* heavenly spirits, trail celestial symbols.

Kwanyin, Chinese, from Northern Honan, Northern Ch'i Dynasty, 565-575 A. D., marble with traces of color, height 68 7/16 inches, Museum purchase, 1952.111.

Bodhisattva, Chinese, Sui Dynasty, 598-618 A. D., limestone, height 32 1/2 inches, Museum purchase, 1950.72.

Horse, Chinese, T'ang Dynasty, 618-907 A. D., glazed pottery, height 20 1/2 inches, Museum purchase, 1950.49.

Kwanyin, Chinese, Sung Dynasty, 960-1280 A. D.,
painted wood, height 38 31/32 inches, Museum
purchase, 1950.73.

Vase, Chinese, Sung Dynasty, 960-1280 A. D.,
glazed pottery, Tz'u Chou ware, height 12 1/8
inches, Museum purchase, 1950.51.

Plate, Chinese, Sung Dynasty, 960-1280 A. D.,
porcelain, Ting yao ware, diameter 7 3/4 inches,
Museum purchase, 1950.55.

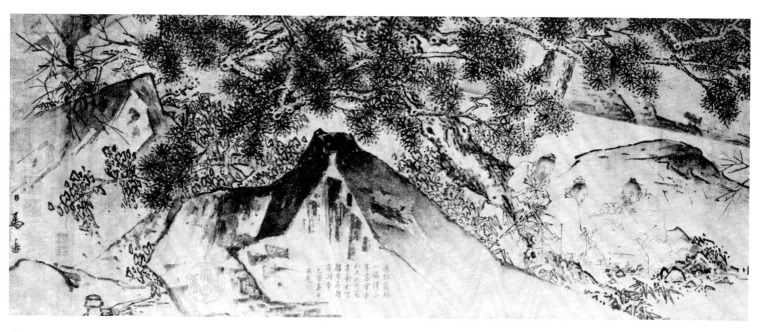

The Four Sages of Shang-Shan (detail) by Ma Yuan, Chinese, active about 1190-1224 A. D., ink and color on paper, 13 1/4 by 121 inches, anonymous gift, 1950.77.

Carpet (detail), North Chinese or Mongolian, XII-XV centuries A. D., knotted wool pile, 25 feet by 17 feet 10 inches, gift of John J. Emery, 1952.241.

Doves and Pear Blossoms after Rain by Ch'ien
Hsüan, Chinese, about 1235-after 1300 A. D., ink
and color on paper, 12 by 38 1/2 inches, The
John J. Emery Fund, 1948.80.

Bamboo by Ku An, Chinese, first half of XIV
century A. D., ink on paper, 44 1/2 by 13 inches,
The John J. Emery Fund, 1948.81.

Birds and Lotus Pond (detail) by Chu-Ta (Pa-Ta Shan-jen), Chinese, active about 1630-1650 A. D., ink on paper, 14 3/4 by 130 inches, Museum purchase, 1950.79.

Urn, (one of a pair), Chinese, Reign of K'ang Hsi, 1662-1722 A. D., porcelain with *bleu fouetté* or *bleu soufflé* glaze, gold patterned overglaze, French gilt bronze mounts, height without plinth 25 7/8 inches, gift of the Duke and Duchess of Talleyrand-Perigord, 1957.506.

Chinese Export Porcelain: From the seventeenth to the end of the nineteenth century, China exported vast quantities of porcelain to Europe and America, much of it decorated with designs sent by the customer with his order. The *Platter,* Ch'ing Dynasty, about 1784-1785 A. D., length 10 inches, gift of William T. Earls, 1958.55, is from a set purchased by George Washington in New York about 1786-1788. It is decorated with a blue Fitzhugh border and an Angel of Fame holding the emblem of the Society of the Cincinnati (an organization of officer veterans of the American Revolutionary army), of which Washington was a charter member. Below the Platter hangs an actual *Badge of the Society of the Cincinnati,* American, late XVIII or early XIX century, metal and enamel, height 1 7/8 inches, gift of William T. Earls, 1968.366. The *Cider Jug,* Ch'ing Dynasty, about 1790, height 11 1/4 inches, gift of Mr. and Mrs. Neil C. Gest, 1955.758, inscribed "Rebellion to Tyrants is Obedience to God," was handed down in the Adams family and is believed to have been presented to President John Adams by Thomas Jefferson.

Japan

Ichikawa Monnosuke II and Onoe Matsuske Visiting Ohisa at the Takashimaya Teahouse by Katsukawa Shunchō, XVIII century A. D., Japanese, color woodcut, early 1790's, 13 13/16 by 9 1/8 inches, Museum purchase, 1912.82.

One Hundred Images of Amida by an unidentified artist, Japanese, XI century A. D., woodcut, 1049 A .D., 18 3/8 by 12 1/8 inches, The Albert P. Strietmann Collection, 1967.1212.

Nichiren Shonin by Un'ichi Hiratsuka, 1895- ,
Japanese, woodcut, 1938, 25 3/8 by 20 inches,
gift of Mr. and Mrs. Howard D. Porter, 1965.431.

Kimono (*Kosode*) with **Underkimono** (*Naga Juban*), Japanese, XVIII or early XIX century A. D., silk damask stencilled and embroidered, underkimono tie-dyed silk, gift of Mr. and Mrs. John J. Emery, 1964.781-782.

Musical Instruments

Man has always made music and lavished his finest crafts on the fashioning of its instruments. The Museum's collection is one of the very few systematic exhibitions of musical instruments in this country, and is based largely on the collection formed by the Cincinnati industrialist Dr. William Howard Doane, himself the composer of many Baptist hymns.

The Asian instruments from China and Japan, Malaya, India and the Near East, many of which are still played today, are arranged by country and shown in their playing positions. So, too, are the Western examples, which trace the evolution of modern keyboard and orchestral instruments without including the well-known modern types.

Western instruments are grouped categorically, including the family of harps and lyres; the plucked lutes in their many variations; bowed lutes from the early spike fiddle to an Amati viola of 1619; horns with fixed pitch, most unusual of them a Roman bronze *buccina* found at Pompeii; horns with variable pitch; the woodwind families of oboes, clarinets, flutes and bassoons. Two of the oldest and nearly universal types of instruments, the bagpipe and hurdy-gurdy, are also represented by comparatively recent examples.

Together they offer a review of human civilization in terms of one artistic medium, which defines visible shapes of sound.

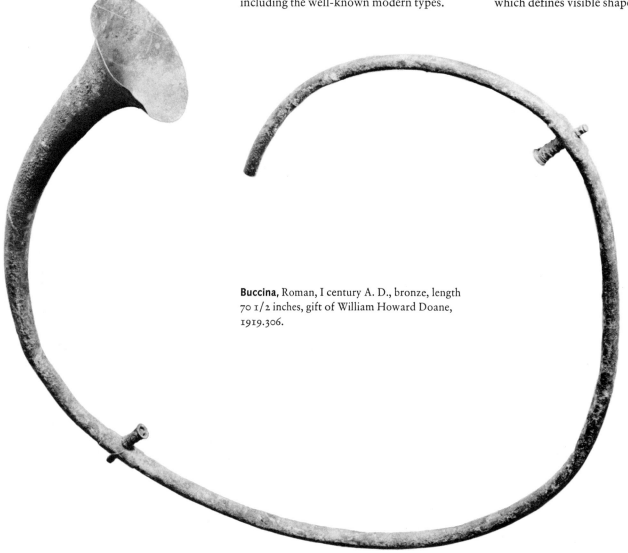

Buccina, Roman, I century A. D., bronze, length 70 1/2 inches, gift of William Howard Doane, 1919.306.

Viola attributed to Nicolo Amati of Cremona, Italy, 1596-1684 A. D., wood, length 27 1/4 inches, gift of Mrs. Peter Gibson, 1911.1911.

Serpent Trumpet, German or Italian, XVI century A. D., wood covered with leather, brass fittings, gift of William Howard Doane, 1914.228.

Virginal, or small rectangular Spinet, by Andreas Ruckers of Antwerp, Flanders, early XVII century A. D., wood case decorated with applied paper, paint and a pewter soundhole rose, width 32 7/8 inches, gift of William Howard Doane, 1914.300.

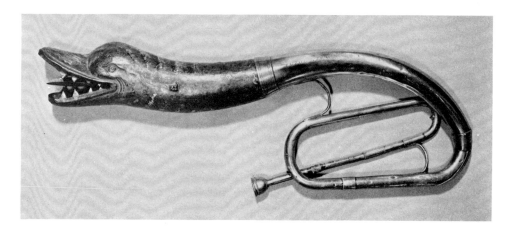

Horn with Dragon Mouth by Calzacci, Rome, XVIII century A. D., brass, length 29 1/2 inches, gift of William Howard Doane, 1919.302.

Lute, XVII century A. D., found in Turkey but probably made in Italy for the Near Eastern market, wood with ivory inlay, length 33 inches, gift of William Howard Doane, 1914.210.

Pianoforte by John Broadwood and Sons, London, England, XVIII century A. D., mahogany case with painted decoration, height 33 inches, gift of Richard Guggenheim, 1958.478.

Oboe D'Amore by Jacob Denner, Nürnberg, Germany, XVIII century A. D., wood with brass fittings, length 26 inches, gift of William Howard Doane, 1919.265.

Lyra Byzantina, Balkan, probably XIX century A. D., wood, tortoise shell and ivory inlay, length 15 1/2 inches, gift of William Howard Doane, 1919.311.

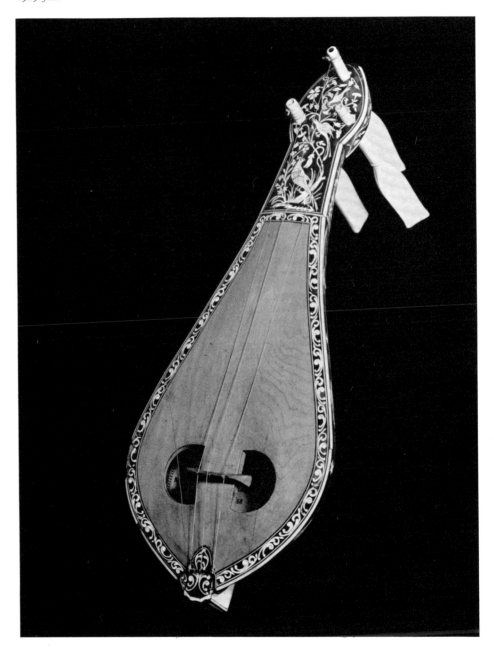

'Ud, Arabian, probably XVIII or XIX century A. D., wood, length 31 inches, gift of William Howard Doane, 1919.249.

This type of instrument which originated in the Middle East gave its characteristic shape and even its name (*al 'Ud* in Arabic) to the European family of Lutes.

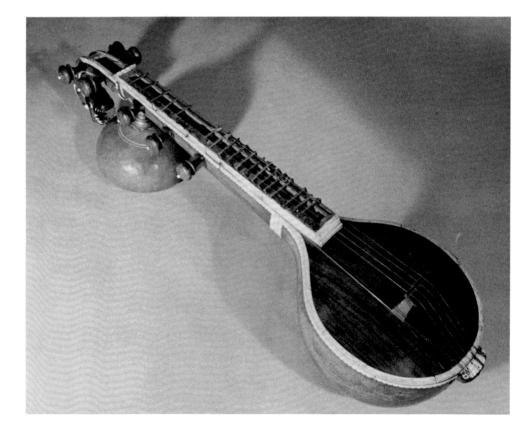

Vina, Indian, probably XIX century A. D., wood and ivory, length 53 inches, gift of William Howard Doane, 1914.303.

This stick-zither with resonating gourd reflects a very ancient design and has an elaborate arrangement of frets to accommodate the complicated scales of Indian music.

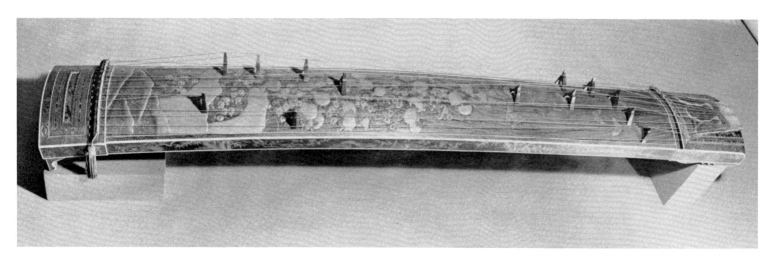

She, Japanese, probably XIX century A. D., lacquered wood inlaid with coral, ivory and shell, length 75 inches, gift of Mr. and Mrs. Charles M. Hinkle, 1891.2956.

This is a Japanese version of a classic Chinese form of long zither persisting from Confucian times to the present in China and Japan.

Shoulder Harp, Burmese, probably XIX century A. D., lacquered wood, brass filigree, skin diaphragm, length 34 inches, gift of William Howard Doane, 1914.43.

Medieval European Art

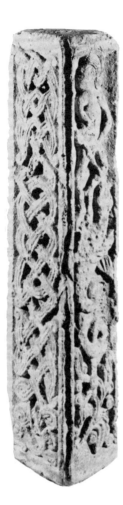

Corner Upright of an Altar Rail, French, probably from the region of Angers, XI century, limestone, height 33 3/4 inches, The George Toewater Fund, 1971.350.

Christianity, the official as well as popular religion of Europe by the end of the fourth century, made seemingly impossible demands on the visual arts. It called on them to depict the invisible, spiritual realities of the new religion. The idealised naturalism of Graeco-Roman style was hardly an appropriate vehicle, but some of its pagan symbols, such as the doves of Venus and the peacocks of Juno, were taken over to represent the soul, the Holy Ghost, immortality. The Chi-Rho, first letters of Christ's name, and the Alpha and Omega of eternity preceded even the cross as central Christian symbols. Human representation came much later, except for a few Hellenistic Mercurys and Apollos disguised as Good Shepherds.

As Christianity spread to Europe from the Eastern Mediterranean, it brought with it the Near East's semi-abstract style to blend with the Western; so, too, the monastic idea came out of Syria and Egypt to take on Roman order and organization. Further adornments came from the northern Celtic and Germanic peoples who on their conversion to Christianity added their complex linear patterns and bright enamel colors to the new alloy.

Architecture gradually was adapted to the needs of Christian worship and the geographic demands which varied from region to region. The cloister arts of ivory-carving, metalwork, and, above all, glorious illuminated manuscripts had achieved a definitive Christian vocabulary by the time that Charlemagne (768 to 814 A. D.) had unified much of Western Europe.

During this time the eastern Christian or Byzantine world, from its capital of Constantinople, was spreading throughout its Greek, Italian and Anatolian domains its own mystical style, climaxed by great domed churches that blazed with brilliant mosaics.

In the eleventh and twelfth centuries Western architecture began to grow in size and artistic importance, while sculptors carved cloister capitals and rich portals for abbeys, cathedrals, and even modest parish churches. Painters decorated every inch of the interiors, and master craftsmen filled the windows with translucent stained and painted glass. This period is called Romanesque, although it had little resemblance to classic Rome.

In the Gothic thirteenth century, sculpture began to free itself from its architectural matrix, and growing specialization of the crafts laid the foundation for the guild system of

Relief with Doves and a Cross, probably Italian, about VII century, later re-used for a memorial inscription in Latin which was cut on the reverse side and dated 1606, limestone, height 12 1/2 inches, Museum purchase, 1973.294.

the later Middle Ages. In sculpture, for example, the "carver" turned his works over to the "whitener" who added the priming coat for the "image maker" or painter. Monumental late twelfth and thirteenth century sculpture, somewhat comparable in spirit and dignity to Archaic Greek sculpture, relaxed in the fourteenth century into a more naturalistic informality, while poses, draperies and other ornaments grew more and more elaborate.

By the fifteenth century tapestries began to take the place of paintings in the church interiors, and the secular architecture of guild halls, townhouses, and government buildings sometimes rivalled the cathedrals in size and richness. Innumerable castles showed the specialized talents of the military architects. Civil unrest and all kinds of warfare being ordinary conditions of life, the armorer's art reached similar heights of distinction.

Christendom and its arts aspired to the unity of its theology, but each region and province and generation modified or enhanced the prevailing style in terms of its own temperament. Thus a marvelous variety of expression thronged the theoretically unified framework of the Middle Ages.

Virgin, French, from the region of Toulouse, about 1130, painted wood, height 34 inches, Museum purchase, 1946.8.

Gargoyle, French, from Poitiers, late XII century, limestone, height 17 1/16 inches, Museum purchase, 1952.15.

Double Capital, Italian, from Piacenza, mid-XII century, limestone, height 10 23/32 inches, gift of Mr. and Mrs. Fletcher Nyce and their friends, 1973.3.

Mural Paintings from the Hermitage of San Baudelio de Berlanga, Province of Soria, Spain, mid-XII century, fresco seco remounted on canvas: *The Falconer,* height 86 5/8 inches, 1962.594; *Meander Border,* height 24 5/16 inches 1962.595; *The Holy Women at the Sepulchre,* height 65 5/16 inches, 1962.599; *St. Nicholas,* height 66 3/4 inches, 1962.600; *Ibis,* height 31 11/16 inches, 1962.598; pair of *Towers,* height 47 9/16 inches, 1962.596-597; pair of *Rampant Wolves Surmounted by Medallions,* height 105 inches, 1964.64-65; Museum purchase and gifts of Elija B. Martindale and The Clowes Fund, Inc.

Capital with Horsemen and Foliage, French, from the region of Toulouse, second half of XII century A. D., limestone, height 11 15/16 inches, Museum purchase, 1973.295.

Tomb Effigy of Don Sancho Saiz Carillo, Spanish, from the Ermita de San Andres, Mahamud, Province of Burgos, 1250-1275, painted and gilded wood, length 92 inches, gift of Mrs. Frederick A. Geier in memory of Emilie Esselborn Crane, 1958.93.

Donor of the Hospice of Salins, French, 1260-1305, limestone, height 69 3/4 inches, The John J. Emery Fund, 1946.7.

Head of a Bishop, Spanish, from Catalonia, XIII century, Urgel stone with traces of paint, height 16 5/8 inches, gift of Piero Tozzi, 1955.745.

Head of an Angel, French, from Rheims, late XIII century, limestone with traces of paint, height 9 1/2 inches, gift of Dikran K. Kelekian, 1948.164.

Virgin and Child, French, mid-XIV century, ivory, height 14 1/2 inches, The John J. Emery Fund, 1971.553.

84

Madonna and Child, Italian, from Siena, 1370-1380, painted wood, height 62 1/2 inches, The Mary Hanna Fund, 1953.151.

Armor of the "Maximilian" Type: Armet-type *Helmet, Cuirass, Hand Guard* (originally attached to a leather gauntlet), named after Maximilian I, Emperor of Austria and the Holy Roman Empire, but made in this style in all the European countries in the XVI century, forged steel, Museum purchase, 1882.2781, .2779, .2778. *Trousse* or Set of Hunting Knives, forged steel, gift of Charles F. Williams, 1952.70-75.

Millefleurs Tapestry, French, XV-XVI century, height 114 1/2 inches, gift of Mrs. Gordon Rentschler, 1973.5.

The escutcheon in the center links this with a set of tapestries from Notre Dame des Ardilliers in Saumur, now in the Tapestry Museum at Angers.

Armor of the "Gothic" Type: *Tilting Shield,* probably German, XVI century, forged steel, 1882. 2786; *Helmet* and *Breast Plate,* probably Italian, XV century, possibly from the workshops of the Missaglia family of Milan, forged steel, Museum purchase, 1882.2776-a, b.

Italian Art

Italy never was sympathetic to the Gothic style of the feudal north. It had produced great Early Christian, Pre-Romanesque and Romanesque arts, but by the thirteenth century it began to stir with new ideas. For one thing, there was a continuity of city life in Italy, inherited from the Romans, which led to a new non-agrarian social structure of trading, manufacturing and banking city-states. Florence was to be the most creative of them, but they were scattered over central and northern Italy, in constant conflict with papal and imperial authority, as well as with local feudal lords.

The plentiful Roman ruins were daily reminders of the classical past, and for a century before Constantinople fell to the Turks in 1453, scholars had begun to arrive with their precious manuscripts and knowledge of the Greek tongue. The excitement of reading Plato and Aristotle in the original brought about a Humanist revolution at the same time the capitalist economy emerged with its emphasis on the material present. The two

ideas combined to create a new scientific and philosophic attitude toward nature and individual man, and the arts were its chief interpreters.

In fact, it has been said that "art was the oxygen of the Renaissance." The Italians thought of all this as a revival of the best of antiquity; hence the word Renaissance, or "rebirth," which identifies the period. Actually, it was the first phase of the modern epoch. Archaeology was invented, anatomy was studied, and painters and sculptors took a fresh look at themselves and the world around them. Painting became the leading art, although sculpture, architecture and the fine crafts, including the new medium of print-making, followed closely. Music began its modern evolution, while the more modern amenities of fine furniture, tableware, and lacemaking set future tastes.

Dante and Giotto were contemporaries in the still half-medieval, half-modern early fourteenth century, and, like all true artists, they summed up the past while predicting

the future. Then, in 1348-49, the Black Death gave sudden importance to the heretofore anonymous common man by drastically reducing the whole population, especially the older generation. Youth took the helm, and the fifteenth century exploded with some of the world's greatest artists as well as writers, philosophers, historians, explorers, and other budding scientists.

It is hard to contain more than a hint of this creative turbulence in one collection. But Fra Angelico and Botticelli of Florence and Mantegna of Mantua and Padua speak for the fifteenth century here; while Leonardo's pupil, Luini, Bronzino, and Annibale Caracci speak for the sixteenth, as do Titian and Tintoretto of Venice. Strozzi follows with the Baroque of the seventeenth century. Venice's long but lovely eighteenth-century twilight can be seen in Canaletto, Bellotto and Tiepolo, all of them far-travelling influences on the rest of European painting.

Esther and Mordecai by Andrea Mantegna, about 1431-1506, oil on canvas, 22 1/8 by 19 1/8 inches, bequest of Mary M. Emery, 1927.406.

Madonna and Child by Fra Angelico (Fra Giovanni da Fiesole, Guido di Pietro da Mugello), 1387-1455, oil on wood, diameter 8 7/8 inches, The Fanny Bryce Lehmer Fund, 1966.267.

Madonna and Child by Mino da Fiesole, 1430/
31-1484, terra cotta, height 49 3/16 inches, working model for the centerpiece of the tomb of
Cardinal Pietro Riario, SS Apostoli, Rome, The
John J. Emery Fund, 1946.4.

Judith with the Head of Holofernes with **Studies
of Animals** on the back, by Botticelli (Alessandro
di Mariano Filipepi), 1444?-1510, tempera on
wood, 11 1/2 by 8 1/2 inches, Museum purchase,
1954.463.

Madonna and Child with Saint John by Francesco
Botticini, 1445-1497, tempera on wood, 20 1/2
by 11 3/4 inches, gift of the Duke and Duchess of
Talleyrand-Perigord, 1956.309.

Sacrifice to Priapus by Jacopo de' Barbari, about 1460/70- about 1511/16, engraving, about 1499-1501, the large version, 9 by 6 5/8 inches, bequest of Herbert Greer French, 1943.104.

Portrait of Philip II by Titian (Tiziano Vecelli), 1477-1576, oil on canvas, 42 3/16 by 36 1/2 inches, bequest of Mary M. Emery, 1927.402.

Moses on Mount Sinai and the Brazen Serpent attributed to Francesco Rosselli, 1448-before 1513, engraving (first state), about 1465-70, 11 3/4 by 17 inches, bequest of Herbert Greer French, 1943.40.

Angel of the Eighth Sphere by the Master of the E-Series Tarocchi, Ferrarese, active about 1465, engraving, 6 5/8 by 3 7/8 inches, bequest of Herbert Greer French, 1943.36.

The Astrologer by Giulio Campagnola, about 1482-1515/17, engraving (second state), 1509, 3 7/8 by 6 inches, bequest of Herbert Greer French, 1943.90.

Madonna and Child with Saint Catherine of Alexandria by Bernardino Luini, about 1481-1532, oil and tempera on canvas, 48 by 38 1/2 inches, bequest of Mary M. Emery, 1927.404.

Hercules and the Nemean Lion by Giovanni Antonio da Brescia, active about 1490-1525, engraving, about 1490-1500, 10 1/4 by 9 1/4 inches, bequest of Herbert Greer French, 1943.100.

Portrait of Eleanor of Toledo and Her Son Ferdinand Dei Medici by Bronzino (Agnolo Allori, Agnolo di Cosimo), 1503-1572, oil on canvas, 45 by 33 inches, bequest of Mary M. Emery, 1927.381.

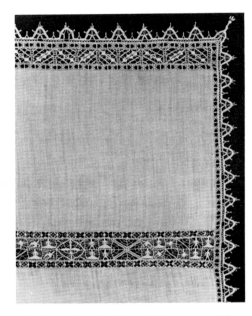

Table Cover (detail), Venice, XVI century, tabby weave linen center with *punto a reticello* (needle-point lace) ends incorporating stylized figures, 72 by 39 inches, gift of the Women's Art Museum Association, 1883.289.

Venus and Adonis by Luca Cambiaso, 1527-1585, pen and wash on paper, 14 1/8 by 9 7/8 inches, gift of Emily Poole, 1953.103.

Majolica Pottery, XVI century: *Albarello* or drug jar, decorated with a portrait, height 8 3/4 inches, gift of Mrs. Daniel H. Holmes, 1923.766. *Tondino* or round dish, in the style of Urbino, inscribed on base, "Mirta 1545," decorated with The Rape of Lucrece, diameter 7 inches, 1950.37; *Tagliera* or trencher, in the style of Urbino, inscribed "Jasonne" in underglaze blue, decorated with Jason and the Golden Fleece, diameter 9 inches, 1956.439; gifts of Dr. and Mrs. J. Louis Ransohoff.

Clytie by Annibale Carracci, 1560-1609, tempera on wood, diameter 17 3/4 inches, gift of the Duke and Duchess of Talleyrand-Perigord, 1952.199.

David with the Head of Goliath by Bernardo Strozzi, 1581-1644, oil on canvas, 60 5/8 by 46 7/8 inches, Museum purchase, 1938.10501.

Circe Changing Ulysses' Men to Beasts by Giovanni Benedetto Castiglione, about 1610-1663/5, etching, early 1650's, 8 9/16 by 12 1/8 inches, The Albert P. Strietmann Collection, 1973.311.

Prison with Numerous Wooden Galleries and a Drawbridge by Giovanni Battista Piranesi, 1720-1778, Plate 7 from *Invenzioni capric di carceri*, etching (first state), late 1740's, 21 3/4 by 16 1/8 inches, bequest of Herbert Greer French, 1943.450.

The Arch of Septimius Severus, Rome, by Canaletto (Giovanni Antonio Canal), 1697-1768, oil on canvas, 20 3/4 by 27 7/8 inches, Museum purchase, 1926.171.

St. Charles Borromeo by Giovanni Battista Tiepolo, 1696-1770, painted for the church of San Pasqual of Baylon, Aranjuez, Spain, oil on canvas, 48 1/8 by 44 1/8 inches, Museum purchase, 1924.178.

Spanish Art

After the Moors had conquered Spain in 711 A. D., its Christian Reconquest was centuries long. But there were peaceful interludes when peoples and their arts mingled. The "Catholic Kings" Ferdinand and Isabella unified the country in 1492, and Spain, under Charles V (1500 to 1558) and Philip II (1527-1598), was master of the New World with its fabulous riches and of much of continental Europe.

In spite of its own distinguished arts, this modern Spain of the Renaissance and early Baroque periods found it convenient or fashionable to import many of its painters. One such was Nicolás Francés who brought in the "International Style" of late Gothic France. The last of them was the Cretan-born,

Venetian-trained El Greco who found his spiritual home in Toledo. Native Spaniards often studied abroad, as Pedro Berruguete did in the Ducal court of Urbino, or were under strong Flemish influence, as were the painters of the Tendilla Retable, or like Lorenzo Zaragoza of Valencia were influenced by Florence and Siena.

The seventeenth century saw a flowering of the Spanish genius, a true "Golden Age" in letters, architecture and especially painting. Philip IV, for example, was an amateur painter himself and a noted patron of many artists, including Zurbarán, Cano and Murillo who set a universal style for the Counter-Reformation Spain so ardently supported. Preeminently there was Velázquez

who was wholly identified with the Spanish court, and who was stylistic ancestor of the nineteenth-century Impressionists.

Spain had already passed the peak of her political and military power by the eighteenth century and was comparatively sterile until in its closing years Goya appeared to record not only the somewhat decadent life of court and town, but also the shock of the Napoleonic invasions and the Spanish people's unexpected heroic resistance. Goya's experiments with the new print medium of lithography were so notable that by the time he died, a self-exile in Bordeaux, these commanded the admiration of a new generation of French artists, headed by Delacroix and Daumier.

The Fall of the Angels by Nicholás Francés, about 1400-1468, oil and tempera on wood, 36 7/8 by 35 1/4 inches, The Fanny Bryce Lehmer Fund, 1959.20.

Retable with Incidents from the Life of St. Peter by Lorenzo Zaragoza, about 1340-about 1420, tempera and gold leaf on wood, 118 by 103 inches, The Edwin and Virginia Irwin Memorial Fund, 1960.473.

The Tendilla Retable by unidentified Spanish and Flemish artists, about 1555-1556, oil on wood, height 144 inches, width with wings open 188 inches, believed to have been commissioned by Inigo Lopez de Mendoza y Figuera, Count Tendilla, for a church near Barcelona, Museum purchase, 1953.219.

Lamentation over the Body of Christ by Pedro Berruguete, about 1450-about 1503, oil and tempera on wood, 41 11/16 by 31 3/4 inches, The Harry S. and Eva Belle Leyman Fund, 1959.19.

Crucifixion with View of Toledo by El Greco
(Domenikos Theotocopoulos), 1547?-1614, oil on
canvas, 41 by 24 3/8 inches, Museum purchase,
1932.5.

The Recovery of the Image of the Virgin of El Puig (St. Peter Nolasco Recovering the Image of the Virgin) by Francisco de Zurbarán, 1598-1664, oil on canvas, 1630 A. D., 64 1/2 by 82 inches, painted for the convent of the Shod Mercedarians, Seville, gift of Mary Hanna, Mr. and Mrs. Charles P. Taft and Stevenson Scott in memory of Charles Frederick Fowles, 1917.58.

Portrait of Philip IV, King of Spain, by Diego Rodriguez de Silva y Velázquez, 1599-1660, oil on canvas, 22 3/16 by 19 7/8 inches, bequest of Mary M. Emery, 1927.425.

Vest, late XVI century, embroidered natural linen with applied cording, gift of the Women's Art Museum Association, 1883.393.

Blind Man Tossed on the Horns of a Bull by Francisco José de Goya y Lucientes, 1746-1828, etching (first state), 5 3/8 by 7 1/8 inches (image), bequest of Herbert Greer French, 1943.527.

St. John the Baptist by Alonso Cano, 1601-1667, oil on canvas, 72 by 44 1/2 inches, painted for the convent of St. Augustine, Seville, The Fanny Bryce Lehmer Fund, 1964.69.

St. Thomas of Villa Nueva Dividing His Clothes among the Beggar Boys by Bartolomé Esteban Murillo, 1617-1682, oil on canvas, about 1670, 86 1/2 by 58 1/2 inches, bequest of Mary M. Emery, 1927.412.

North European Art: Fifteenth to Eighteenth Centuries

While the arts of Renaissance Italy matured into a spacious pageantry, greater forces of change such as the Reformation, the rise of the modern state, and the birth of experimental science were shaking the countries of Northern Europe. In the Middle Ages a society of "free" trading, manufacturing and banking cities had developed in the Germanies and especially in the Flemish Lowlands. By the beginning of the fifteenth century they, like the Italian city-states, were producing arts of the greatest distinction, and as in Italy painting took the lead. But in contrast to the open Mediterranean skies and amiable climate of Italy, the dense northern forests and long, snowy, often fog-bound winters inclined painting toward a minute and detailed realism.

The second generation of fifteenth century northern artists boasted such stellar names as Hans Memling, Dieric Bouts and his circle, and some of the early masters of the print. The printing press was a northern invention, changing the entire history of civilization and the structure of society by opening new worlds of communication. Before enough books were available for literacy to become general, the graphic arts of etching, learned originally from the armorers, and engraving on metal and wood had been instruments of popular education and propaganda, especially in the north.

The early sixteenth century brought increased contact with the classic south, broadening northern style into the masterpieces of Albrecht Dürer of Nuremberg, his follower Georg Pencz, the later Adriaen Isenbrandt, Joos van Cleve and Lucas Cranach, official painter to the Lutheran Reformation. The new scientific attitude toward nature led to landscape painting as an end in itself, as with Herri Met de Bles, stylistic descendant of the great Brueghel.

The modern period came of age in the Baroque seventeenth century of Flanders and Holland. The opposed temperaments of Rubens and Rembrandt were its chief exemplars. Portrait painting thrived in the hands of Anthony van Dyck, Frans Hals, Nicolaes Maes and many others. Specialization created a school of genre painters, recorders of daily life, with Ter Borch and de Hooch as its outstanding masters. There were still-life specialists such as Isaak Soreau, and landscape specialists like Jacob van Ruisdael, Hobbema, Aert van der Neer, and Van der Heyden who were major artists by any standards.

Naturally, the fine crafts necessary to comfortable, sometimes luxurious private life flourished, as middle-class, town-dwelling manufacturers and merchants gradually supplemented the old feudal aristocracy as patrons for all the arts.

It was, however, under the royal patronage of Augustus the Strong, Elector of Saxony and King of Poland, that Johan Friedrich Boettger succeeded, between 1708 and 1710, in duplicating the formula for porcelain, kaolin clay and petuntze, or china stone, which, until then, was a secret known only to the Chinese (porcelain is still popularly known as "china"). This was an outstanding achievement, since Chinese porcelain, which was considerably superior to European pottery, was enormously popular in Europe and had been imported in ever-increasing quantities since the early seventeenth century.

St. Stephen and St. Christopher by Hans Memling, Flemish, about 1433-1494, pair of wing panels of a triptych, oil and tempera on wood, 18 23/32 by 6 3/16 inches, gift of Mrs. E. W. Edwards, 1956.11, 1955.793.

These panels were once part of a small altarpiece with an arched panel in the center, recently identified tentatively as a *Flight into Egypt,* now in a private collection in Paris. The pair of shutters that closed over the center panel had St. Stephen and St. Christopher on their outer faces and a St. John the Baptist and a Mary Magdalen, now in the Louvre, on their inner faces.

The Adoration of the Magi by a follower of Dieric Bouts, Flemish, late XV century, oil and tempera on wood, 36 1/2 by 52 inches, bequest of Mary M. Emery, 1927.380.

St. Jerome in His Study by Albrecht Dürer,
German, 1471-1528, engraving, 1514, 9 5/8 by
7 3/8 inches, bequest of Herbert Greer French,
1943.205.

Head of a Woman by Adriaen Isenbrandt,
Flemish, died 1551, oil and tempera on wood,
9 7/8 by 7 7/8 inches, Museum purchase, 1962.67.

St. Helena, Mother of Constantine, by Lucas Cranach the Elder, German, 1472-1553, oil on wood, 1525, 16 by 10 5/8 inches, bequest of Mary M. Emery, 1927.387.

Portrait of Francis I, King of France, by Joos van Cleve, Flemish, 1490-1540, oil on wood, 28 3/8 by 23 1/4 inches, bequest of Mary M. Emery, 1927.384.

Landscape with Sacrifice of Abraham by Herri Met de Bles, Flemish, 1480-1550, oil on wood, 22 1/8 by 33 7/8 inches, The Fanny Bryce Lehmer Fund, 1944.44.

SEINES ALTERS XXXIIII · IAR

A Knight in Armor by Georg Pencz, German, 1500-1550, oil on wood, 15 3/4 by 13 3/4 inches, bequest of Mary M. Emery, 1927.392.

Castle on an Island by Augustin Hirschvogel, German, 1503-1553, etching, 1546, 3 by 5 7/8 inches, bequest of Herbert Greer French, 1943.238.

The Last Supper by Crispin van den Broeck, Dutch, 1524-1591, chiaroscuro woodcut and etching, 9 1/4 by 9 5/16 inches, gift of Herbert Greer French, 1940.612.

Samson and Delilah by Peter Paul Rubens, Flemish, 1577-1640, oil on wood, about 1609, 20 1/2 by 19 7/8 inches, *modello* for the painting formerly in the Rockox collection and now in a private collection in Hamburg, The Harry S. and Eva Belle Leyman Fund, 1972.459.

Town with Four Towers by Hercules Seghers, Dutch, 1589/90-about 1638, hand-colored etching and drypoint on green wash, 7 7/8 by 12 3/4 inches, bequest of Herbert Greer French, 1943.344.

A Dutch Family by Frans Hals, Dutch, 1584-1666, oil on canvas, 44 1/2 by 36 3/4 inches, bequest of Mary M. Emery, 1927.399.

Portrait of a Member of the Balbi Family by Anthony van Dyck, Flemish, 1599-1641, oil on canvas, 52 1/4 by 47 1/4 inches, bequest of Mary M. Emery, 1927.393.

Winter Landscape by Aert van der Neer, Dutch, 1603?-1677, oil on canvas, 23 by 27 1/2 inches, gift of Audrey Emery, 1953.1.

Still Life with Dish of Strawberries by Isaak Soreau, German-Flemish, 1604-after 1638, tempera on wood, 11 1/2 by 16 inches, gift of Mrs. Robert McKay, 1960.496.

Young Girl Holding a Medal by Rembrandt Harmensz. van Rijn, Dutch, 1606-1669, oil on canvas, 25 7/8 by 22 7/8 inches, bequest of Mary M. Emery, 1927.415.

A Music Party by Gerard Ter Borch, Dutch,
1617-1681, oil on wood, 22 7/8 by 18 5/8 inches,
bequest of Mary M. Emery, 1927.421.

Faust in His Study by Rembrandt Harmensz.
van Rijn, Dutch, 1606-1669, etching and drypoint
(first state), 1652, 8 1/4 by 6 3/8 inches, bequest
of Herbert Greer French, 1943.315.

The Game of Skittles by Pieter de Hooch, Dutch, 1629-after 1684, oil on canvas, 29 1/8 by 26 1/8 inches, gift of Mary Hanna, 1950.19.

Scene in Westphalia by Jacob van Ruisdael, Dutch, 1628-1682, oil on canvas, 40 1/4 by 49 5/8 inches, gift of Mary Hanna, 1946.98.

Portrait of Titus Rembrandt by Nicolaes Maes,
Dutch, 1632-1693, oil on canvas, about 1650,
29 1/8 by 23 3/4 inches, gift of Mary Hanna,
1946.95.

Kas or Cupboard, Dutch, probably from
Friesland, XVII century, oak, height 80 inches,
gift of Mr. and Mrs. Lucien Wulsin, 1951.295.

A Canal in Vecht by Jan van der Heyden, Dutch, 1637-1712, oil on wood, 18 5/8 by 22 1/2 inches, gift of Mary Hanna, 1946.93.

Tankard by Johan Friedrich Boettger, German, 1682-1719, red stoneware, about 1708-1709, Royal Saxon Factory at Meissen, height 10 9/16 inches with thumbpiece, The Mr. and Mrs. Arthur Joseph Collection, 165.1932.

Eighteenth-Century German Glazed Pottery: *Coffeepot,* from Ansbach, about 1735, height 11 1/2 inches, 1961.318; *Jug,* from Fulda, about 1745, height 9 inches, 1961.319; *Covered Tureen,* from Hoechst, about 1750, marked with a Z (probably for decorator Johannes Zeschinger) and a six-spoke wheel in overglaze black, height 9 1/2 inches, 1961.316; gifts of the Duke and Duchess of Talleyrand-Perigord.

Flight into Egypt, from the workshop of Couly Nouailher, Limoges, XVI century, enamel on copper, 11 1/4 by 7 3/4 inches, gift of Dr. and Mrs. J. Louis Ransohoff, 1950.36.

The Triumph of the Unicorn by Jean Duvet, 1485-after 1561, engraving, 9 1/4 by 15 1/2 inches, bequest of Herbert Greer French, 1943.176.

French Art: Sixteenth to Mid-Nineteenth Centuries

France welcomed the Renaissance with open arms, even while its native Gothic arts were reaching an ornate climax. The following *détente,* or relaxation, of the early sixteenth century could be called either the last medieval phase or the first modern phase of French art. French kings invaded a defenseless Italy, bringing back a booty of artists as well as works of art. Flemish masters were eagerly imported as official portrait painters. The famous chateaux of the Loire Valley, no longer military castles, rose in a rich and fascinating confusion of styles .

Francis I (1494-1547) had brought Leonardo da Vinci to France, to be followed by a succession of Italian artists established at Fontainebleau. It became the productive center as well as the School of French Renaissance art during the turmoil of the religious wars and the consolidation of royal authority in that period. By the seventeenth century, however, France had achieved full modern nationhood, with the inevitable result of achieving a national style in the arts.

Some of its early masters, like Claude of Lorraine, preferred the classic calm of Italy to the pushy materialism of the new France, and the newly-founded French Academy maintained a branch in Rome. Other seventeenth-century painters such as Vouet, who was First Painter to King Louis XIII (1601 to 1643), returned from Italian training to teach a whole generation of painters, decorators, even landscape architects who adorned the long and splendid reign of Louis XIV (1643-1715).

On this solid Baroque foundation, France entered the Rococo eighteenth century as the artistic dictator of Europe. The short-lived but brilliant Watteau heads the roll call of painters, followed by Nattier and Boucher, arbiter of elegance for Louis XV (1717-1774) and Madame de Pompadour, and finally Fragonard, his friend Hubert Robert, and Vigée-Lebrun, one of the foremost women painters. They all had many followers and disciples.

Architecture and its attendant decorative arts, after accomplishing their seventeenth-century masterpiece at Versailles, flourished abundantly, as did letters and music in its new forms of opera and ballet.

Painters like Fragonard and Boucher executed designs for the great tapestry houses like Gobelins and Beauvais, where they were woven into magnificent wall hangings and even coverings for upholstered furniture for the royal palaces. Their designs were also executed in the so-called soft paste porcelain, a brilliant imitation of true porcelain, available after 1673, which the French ceramic factories, in their efforts to reproduce Chinese porcelain, achieved by mixing glass-making materials with their clay.

This late afternoon of the "Old Regime" was alive with new social and political ideas of the utmost importance. The master sculptor Houdon portrayed some of the leaders, as he did several of the founding fathers of the revolutionary United States. When the French Revolution (1789-1804 including the Directorate and Consulate) violently introduced a new era, David was its official painter, continuing in that role for Napoleon's Empire (1804-1815). Ingres followed him, stressing the Academy's emphasis on drawing and painting in the tradition of the High Renaissance.

Delacroix and his fellow Romantics strongly influenced by the contemporary writings of Byron, Scott, Goethe and a revived interest in Shakespeare, reacted against the new Classicism; static and lifeless it seemed to them. In 1830 further social unrest stimulated by the Industrial Revolution led a group of artists to the village of Barbizon in the Forest of Fontainebleau to seek out unspoiled nature and the common tiller of the soil, to see and paint them freshly. Dupré, Théodore Rousseau and Millet were the vanguard of the movement, and Daubigny was most important of the many followers. Paralleling it was Corot, who began in the manner of David and graduated into one of the finest landscape and figure styles of the period. Courbet added his own blunt "Realism." Corot's friend, Daumier, stayed on in Paris and its environs, drawing his famous lithograph cartoons at night to save precious daylight for his often unfinished paintings. It was one of the greatest epochs in French art, pregnant with a great future.

Bacchus, molded oval dish, by Bernard Palissy, about 1510-1590, polychrome glazed pottery, 8 1/8 by 10 1/2 inches, gift of Dr. and Mrs. J. Louis Ransohoff, 1953.223.

The Artist Studying from Nature by Claude Gelée (called le Lorrain), 1600-1682, oil on canvas, 1639, 30 3/4 by 39 3/4 inches, gift of Mary Hanna, 1946.102.

Lycian Farmers Turned into Frogs, tapestry, woven at the Gobelins factory, Paris, 1601-1627, with the Gobelins marks of Frans van den Planken (François de la Planche) of Oudenaarde and Marc de Comans of Brussels, cartoons attributed to Toussaint Dubreuil, 1561-1602, 162 by 142 inches, one of a set of five showing myths of Diana, gift of Mr. and Mrs. Harry S. Leyman, 1942.99.

The Toilet of Venus by Simon Vouet, 1590-1649, oil on canvas, 72 3/8 by 60 1/4 inches, The Fanny Bryce Lehmer Fund, 1970.459.

Henri IV Room, painted wood panels with inset paintings on canvas, about 1608-1610, gift of Susan D. Bliss, 1957.486.

The wood panels of walls and ceiling are decorated in the style of Fontainebleau with flowers, scrolls, palmettes, the crowned-H cipher of Henri IV, the interlaced L's of the Dauphin, later Louis XIII, and illustrations after the *Amorum Emblemata, Figuris Aeneis Incisa,* published in 1608 by Otto van Veen of Antwerp under whom Rubens studied. The inset paintings illustrate the story of Amintas and Sylvia from the poem *Aminta* by the Italian, Torquato Tasso, which was published in 1573.

Study of Hands and a Bodice by Antoine Watteau, 1684-1721, red, black and white chalk on paper, 7 by 8 inches, gift of Mr. and Mrs. Lucien Wulsin, 1928.2.

Salon of the Régence Period, about 1715-1723, carved oak panels with inset mirrors and chinoiserie paintings, gift of Mrs. Herbert N. Straus, 1958.256.

This room, probably from a noble residence in Paris, reflects the transition that occurred during the minority of Louis XV from the monumental style of the reign of Louis XIV to the Rococo of the mid-eighteenth century. The overdoor paintings may have been added as much as twenty years after the panels were carved.

Portrait of Mme. Thérèse de la Martinière by
Jean-Marc Nattier, 1685-1766, oil on canvas,
1729, 32 by 25 3/4 inches, bequest of Mary M.
Emery, 1927.413.

Louis XV Room, carved, painted and gilded wood
panels, about 1750, gift of the Duke and
Duchess of Talleyrand-Perigord, 1955.796;
Mantel, red marble, gift of Mrs. James M.
Hutton, 1964.186.

The paintings that decorate the panels are
attributed to Christophe Huet who died in 1759,
and are related to *Singeries ou différentes actions
de la vie humaine représentées par des singes
dediées au public gravées sur les dessins de C.
Huet par J. Guelard.*

The Water Mill by François Boucher, 1703-1770,
oil on canvas, 1764, 24 by 32 inches, gift of
Mary Hanna, 1935.264.

Chinese Fishing Scene, Beauvais tapestry, about
1750, based on an oil sketch by François Boucher,
1703-1770, cartoons by Dumont, 144 by 105
inches, The John J. Emery Fund, 1945.10.

Several sets of eight tapestries based on
"Chinese" sketches by Boucher were woven at
Beauvais. One set was sent to the Emperor of
China by Louis XV, and another set is reputed
to have been woven for Mme. de Pompadour.
Cincinnati's tapestry is approximately one-half
its original width, the acanthus borders having
been added after it was divided.

The Education of Love, Sèvres biscuit or un-glazed soft paste, modeled by Etienne-Maurice Falconet after a drawing by Boucher, 1763, height 13 1/4 inches, gift of the Duke and Duchess of Talleyrand-Perigord, 1954.523.

The Letter by Jean-Honoré Fragonard, 1732-1806, oil on canvas, 15 by 11 5/8 inches, gift of Mary Hanna, 1946.101.

The Education of the Children, Beauvais tapestry, believed to be based on watercolor sketches by Jean-Honoré Fragonard, 1732-1806, cartoons attributed to François Casanova, signed "ACC Beauvais" for André Charlemagne Charron, Director at Beauvais 1778-1780, 127 1/2 by 80 inches, 1960.559, one of a set of four tapestries, gifts of the Duke and Duchess of Talleyrand-Perigord, John W. Warrington, Joseph B. Hall and John J. Emery.

This set of tapestries was woven for Louis XVI to present to Louis Bénigne de Bertier de Sauvigny, Intendant de Paris, on the occasion of the marriage of the latter's eldest daughter. The figures represent members of de Bertier de Sauvigny's family.

The Glade by Hubert Robert, 1733-1808, oil on canvas, 67 3/4 by 39 inches, gift of the Duchess of Talleyrand-Perigord, John J. Emery, Audrey Emery, Mrs. Robert McKay and Thomas Emery, 1962.13.

Costumes of the Third Quarter of the Eighteenth Century: Left, embroidered silk voided-velvet *Coat,* embroidered satin *Waistcoat,* satin *Breeches,* gift of Mrs. R. M. Hollingshead, 1915.481-483. Center, *Gown* of gold net and lace over gold brocade, possibly Italian, gift of Mrs. Robert McKay, 1963.817. Right, silver-embroidered silk velvet *Coat* and *Breeches,* silk rep *Waistcoat,* gift of Mrs. R. M. Hollingshead, 1915.478-480.

Salon of the Reign of Louis XVI, about 1785, carved, painted and gilded wood panels with inset mirrors and inset grisaille-painted canvas panels, windows, doors and a marble and gilt-bronze mantel, gift of Mrs. Alfred Anson, 1945.73.

The architectural elements of this room from a house in Paris, probably one of those pulled down in the early nineteenth century to make space for Hausmann's boulevards, are decorated in the neo-classic style with a Rococo element persisting in the garlands over the mirrors. The *Beauvais Tapestry Covers* on the suite of chairs and settee (1952.377-384) are based on designs by Oudry executed as early as 1736. The signed *Table* (1949.143) by Charles Topino, who was active in Paris from 1730-1798, combines marquetry chinoiseries with gilt bronze mounts based largely on classical motifs.
Gift of Mrs. Anson.

Portrait of Jean Jacques Rousseau by Jean
Antoine Houdon, 1741-1828, plaster, 1778,
height 27 3/16 inches, gift of John J. Emery,
1944.104.

Portrait of a Young Girl by Jacques Louis David,
1748-1825, oil on canvas, 1788, inscribed on the
back, "Mlle. Scia," 29 by 23 1/2 inches, The
John J. Emery Fund, 1917.369.

The Poorly Defended Rose by Philibert Louis
Debucourt, 1755-1832, etching, roulette and
aquatint (first state), 1791, 16 1/2 by 13 1/8
inches, bequest of Herbert Greer French,
1943.421.

Portrait of Mme. de Fries by Marie Louise
Elisabeth Vigée-Lebrun, 1755-1842, oil on canvas,
about 1792-4, 35 by 28 1/2 inches, gift of Emilie
L. Heine in memory of Mr. and Mrs. John
Hauck, 1940.981.

Portrait of Cherubini by Jean Auguste Dominique
Ingres, 1780-1867, oil on canvas, 1841, 32 3/8 by
28 inches, bequest of Mary M. Emery, 1927.386.

Portrait of Captain Faulte du Puyparlier by Jean
Baptiste Camille Corot, 1796-1875, oil on canvas,
1829, 25 1/2 by 21 1/2 inches, bequest of Emilie
L. Heine, 1956.227.

Ruins of the Chateau of Pierrefonds by Jean Baptiste Camille Corot, 1796-1875, oil on canvas, 29 1/2 by 42 inches, gift of Emilie L. Heine in memory of Mr. and Mrs. John Hauck, 1940.965.

Medea Slaying the Children of Jason by Ferdinand Victor Eugène Delacroix, 1798-1863, oil on canvas, 43 1/2 by 33 inches, gift of John W. Warrington, 1950.303.

Orchestra Stalls by Honoré Daumier, 1808-1879, oil on canvas, 23 13/16 by 33 1/4 inches, The Edwin and Virginia Irwin Memorial Fund, 1960.22.

Liberté de la Presse—Ne Vous y Frottez Pas (Freedom of the Press. Don't Meddle with It) by Honoré Daumier, 1808-1879, plate 20 from *L'Association Mensuelle,* lithograph, 1834, 12 by 17 inches, bequest of Elsie Holmes Warrington, 1941.126.

Going to Work by Jean-François Millet, 1814-1875, oil on canvas, 1851, 22 by 18 inches, bequest of Mary M. Emery, 1927.411.

Plateau de Belle-Croix, Forest of Fontainebleau, by Jules Dupré, 1811-1889, oil on canvas, 1830, 68 by 58 inches, bequest of Mary M. Emery, 1927.391.

Valley of Tiffauge by Théodore Rousseau, 1812-1867, oil on canvas, about 1837-44, 25 1/2 by 40 1/2 inches, gift of Emilie L. Heine in memory of Mr. and Mrs. John Hauck, 1940.1202.

The Pond of Gylieu by Charles F. Daubigny,
1817-1878, oil on canvas, 1853, 24 1/2 by 39 1/4
inches, gift of Emilie L. Heine in memory of Mr.
and Mrs. John Hauck, 1940.969.

The Forest in Winter by Gustave Courbet, 1819-
1877, oil on canvas, 27 1/2 by 43 inches, The
John J. Emery Fund, 1913.12.

The Small Bridge by Charles Meryon, 1821-1868,
etching (third state), 1850, 10 1/4 by 7 3/8 inches,
bequest of Herbert Greer French, 1943.614.

Shawl (detail), XIX century, silk Chantilly lace,
triangular, 104 by 58 inches, bequest of Mary
Dexter, 1912.306.

Jacobean Interior: *The Chimneypiece,* possibly from Bristol, early XVII century, Bath limestone, is decorated with an escutcheon, allegorical representations of The Five Senses, supporting figures, trophies, etc., height 13 feet, gift of The Crosley Foundation, 1963.406. Shown with it are furnishings appropriate to a prosperous English seventeenth-century household, many of which would be imports from the Continent. The *Wainscot Chair* (1962.709), paneled *Settle* (1962.719) and carved *Chest* (1962.708), gifts of Page Crosley Kess, exhibit the style of the early seventeenth century which persisted throughout the century, particularly in areas remote from London. The *Portrait of a Woman* (1889.851), Museum purchase, is probably by a Dutch painter, since many of the painters active in England in the sixteenth and seventeenth centuries were of Dutch origin.

Morning by William Hogarth, 1697-1764, from *Times of Day,* engraving and etching, 1738, 19 1/4 by 15 1/2 inches, gift of Emily Poole, 1955.344.

British Art: Seventeenth to Mid-Nineteenth Centuries

After several centuries of producing a distinguished but somewhat isolated Medieval art, Renaissance England's appetite for new continental styles and decorative motives, chiefly from Italy and the Lowlands, seemed insatiable and often unselective. Painters and sculptors were imported wholesale, and even the native English genius for architecture with its garniture and embellishment sometimes seems as rich, profuse, and disordered as an Elizabethan drama. Yet there are possibly no masterpieces in the world comparable to the great English houses of the sixteenth and seventeenth centuries—small palaces they frequently were—with their furnishings, gardens, and perfect sense of site. And this genius was even stronger in the eighteenth century.

Britain never had lacked for poets and writers of all kinds, but not much painting of more than local consequence developed until this same eighteenth century. While it was a time of great technological and scientific change, prelude to the Industrial Revolution, its essentially decorative arts were scaled to the taste and portrayal of cultivated individuals rather than to the statement of powerful ideas. Nevertheless, its painting was the exact instrument to record the privileged world of the British aristocracy. Country mansions and town houses overflowed with portraits and conversation pieces; the subjects were memorable, but the quality uneven.

One reason for this happy union of subject and artist was that the artists were at last accepted as social equals. Several of them, beginning with Sir Joshua Reynolds, first President of the Royal Academy, and including Raeburn and Lawrence were knighted, an honor previously reserved for foreign celebrities like Rubens, Van Dyck and Lely.

Gainsborough, Reynolds and Romney belong to the long lifetime of George III (1738 to 1820), whereas Hoppner and Lawrence were almost official painters to the Regency (1811 to 1820). William Blake, one of the most original painter-poet-mystics of any time or place and precursor of the modern Surrealists, belongs to both the eighteenth and nineteenth centuries.

Gainsborough thought of himself as primarily a painter of "land-skips," and it was logical that the lyric instinct of British poetry should eventually find its equivalent in landscape painting, especially in the early nineteenth century art of John Constable. Turner was a little later to develop, and powerfully affected not only the Impressionists but also many artists of the second half of the twentieth century. Constable, Blake and Turner are perhaps the only British artists who have significantly influenced the main current of European painting in their own or later times.

Britannia, from the Longton Hall ceramic factory, Staffordshire, porcelain, about 1759, height 15 1/2 inches, gift of The Museum Shop Committee and Volunteers, 1973.107.

Portrait of William, Viscount Pulteney, by Sir Joshua Reynolds, 1723-1792, oil on canvas, probably about 1762, 36 1/2 by 28 1/4 inches, gift of Mr. and Mrs. Albert P. Strietmann, 1953.330.

English Silver: *Tankard* by Thomas Wynne, London, 1776-1777, gift of Nancy and Mary G. Sheerer in memory of Leila Hall and William Anderson Hall, 1936.838. *Tankard* by John Sutton, London, 1684-1685, gift of the Duke and Duchess of Talleyrand-Perigord, 1952.208. *Shaving Bowl,* London, 1713-1714, gift of the Duke and Duchess of Talleyrand-Perigord, 1956.297.

Portrait of Mrs. Philip Thicknesse (Ann Ford) by Thomas Gainsborough, 1727-1788, oil on canvas, about 1760, 77 5/8 by 53 1/8 inches, bequest of Mary M. Emery, 1927.396.

The Cottage Door by Thomas Gainsborough, 1727-1788, oil on canvas, 48 1/4 by 58 3/4 inches, given in honor of Mr. and Mrs. Charles F. Williams by their children, 1948.173.

Eighteenth-Century Room, carved and painted pine, gift of Mrs. Herbert N. Straus, 1955.525.

The rediscovery of Greek and Roman architecture in the mid-eighteenth century inspired most of the decoration of this room: the curving broken pediments, scrolls, masks, acanthus leaves, cornice and decorative moldings. The upholstered *Wing Chair* (1961.153) and little round *Table* with inlaid top (1960.3), gifts of Mrs. J. Louis Ransohoff, the *Side Chairs* (1956.355-356), gift of William Chatfield, the *Kettle Table* (1962.338), gift of Mrs. J. Louis Ransohoff and Charles Fleischmann, all conform to the elegant styles broadcast to all parts of England and to the American colonies through Thomas Chippendale's *The Gentleman and Cabinet-Maker's Director,* first published in 1754 and reprinted numerous times. The Far Eastern trade which made so many English fortunes is reflected in the Chinese *Carved Rhinoceros Horn* (1910.37), gift of Erasmus Gest, in the Korean *Lacquer Stand* (1955.541), gift of Mrs. Robert McKay, and in the *Portrait of William Frankland,* son of one of the Governors of Bengal, painted by Mather Brown, 1761-1831, an American who moved to England after the Revolution, gift of Alexander F. Anderson, 1945.48.

Elizabeth, Duchesss-Countess of Sutherland, by
George Romney, 1734-1802, oil on canvas, 1782,
30 1/2 by 25 1/4 inches, given in honor of Mr.
and Mrs. Charles F. Williams by their children,
1948.172.

The Adam Style: *Pair of Chairs,* painted wood
with caned seats, late eighteenth century, part of
a set of which other pieces are in the Royal Collection, England, gift of Mrs J. Louis Ransohoff,
1960.4-5. *Console Table,* carved and painted
wood with inlaid marble top, late eighteenth
century, gift of Mrs. J. Louis Ransohoff, 1961.117.
Mirror, back-painted and gilded, early eighteenth
century, gift of the Duke and Duchess of Talleyrand-Perigord, 1958.521.

The Duchess of Rutland by Valentine Green,
1739-1813, after Sir Joshua Reynolds, 1723-1792,
mezzotint (first state), 1780, 25 by 15 1/4 inches,
bequest of Herbert Greer French, 1943.463.

The Elphinstone Children by Sir Henry Raeburn,
1756-1823, oil on canvas, 78 by 60 1/2 inches,
bequest of Mary M. Emery, 1927.414.

Master John Turing by John Hoppner, 1758-1810, oil on canvas, 50 by 40 inches, bequest of Harry S. and Eva Belle Leyman, 1943.8.

Portrait of Mrs. Francis Gregg and Her Son, Master George Gregg, by Sir Thomas Lawrence, 1769-1830, oil on canvas, 50 by 40 inches, bequest of Mary M. Emery, 1927.403.

Dress, yellow silk taffeta with cream silk braid, about 1825-1829, gift of Mrs. E. E. Hardcastle in memory of Edward E. Hardcastle, 1948.165.

Coblentz by Joseph Mallord William Turner,
1775-1851, watercolor on paper, 1841-42,
11 15/16 by 18 3/8 inches, bequest of Mary
Hanna, 1956.112.

Waterloo Bridge by John Constable, 1776-1837,
oil on canvas, about 1824, 21 11/16 by 30 11/16
inches, gift of Mary Hanna, 1946.109.

The Lonely Tower by Samuel Palmer, 1805-1881,
crayon and wash on paper, 8 by 11 1/4 inches,
gift of Emily Poole, 1953.82.

St. Etienne du Mont and the Pantheon, Paris, by
Thomas Shotter Boys, 1803-1874, from *Pictur-
esque Architecture in Paris, Ghent . . .* , 1839,
color lithograph, 13 7/8 by 11 3/8 inches, gift of
Albert P. Strietmann, 1954.232.

Cotton Mather by Peter Pelham, 1684/1697-1751 (born in Britain), mezzotint (first state), about 1728, 13 3/4 by 10 inches, bequest of Herbert Greer French, 1943.376.

Portrait of Robert Wilmot by John Singleton Copley, 1737-1815, oil on canvas, probably about 1758, 15 by 11 1/4 inches, The Edwin and Virginia Irwin Memorial Fund, 1967.41.

Portrait of Philip Francis by John Hesselius, 1728-1778, oil on canvas, probably about 1760, 30 by 25 inches, The Edwin and Virginia Irwin Memorial Fund, 1966.30.

Ophelia and Laertes by Benjamin West, 1738-1820, oil on canvas, about 1792, 109 by 152 1/2 inches, gift of Joseph Longworth, 1882.230.

American Art: Eighteenth to Mid-Nineteenth Centuries

American art in the eighteenth century was understandably colonial, but not entirely English colonial. The promise of the new land with its elbow room for dissidents and opportunists of many kinds had attracted a varied and colorful population. The founding of the new independent Republic brought a flood of immigration which continued in growing force well into the twentieth century. Adapting to the new physical conditions, these newcomers in turn adapted their inherited crafts and folk arts into something distinctively different.

John Hesselius of Swedish ancestry and John Singleton Copley of English Boston speak for the painting of the colonial period. Native-born Charles Willson Peale and John Trumbull both served in the Revolutionary army and, like many of the founders, were versatile and ingenious men. But with a strongly felt need for better artistic training than America could provide, artists like Gilbert Stuart of Rhode Island and the Philadelphia Quaker Benjamin West went to England, as had Copley and Trumbull. West even became the second President of the Royal Academy.

As the nineteenth century advanced, later painters such as Fitz Hugh Lane, Aaron Corwine and Miner Kellogg developed an indefinable but definitely indigenous quality. Some, George Caleb Bingham and C. T. Webber, for example, addressed themselves to specific historical subjects; others like John Mix Stanley painted Indians. Thomas Cole, Asher Durand, Frederic Church, Robert Duncanson and Worthington Whittredge were fascinated by the American landscape, often travelling west with the frontier. There were sculptors too, who like Hiram Powers originally worked only in marble in their Italian studios, or like the later Randolph Rogers worked in bronze as well as marble.

Architecture and the decorative arts also acquired an American accent through the Federal and Classic Revival periods, expressing, as they inevitably must, the society and economy, the total culture that called them into being. Sydney Smith might ask in 1820, "In the four quarters of the globe, who reads an American book, or goes to an American play, or looks at an American picture or statue?" The answer is simple, almost chauvinistically simple: Americans read American books, looked at American pictures and statues, and continue to do so with growing interest as the rest of the world is beginning to.

Portrait of Francis Bailey, Portrait of Mrs. Francis Bailey, by Charles Willson Peale, 1741-1827, oil on canvas, 26 by 21 3/4 inches, The Edwin and Virginia Irwin Memorial Fund, 1957.146-147.

The Sortie from Gibraltar by John Trumbull,
1756-1843, oil on canvas, 1788, 20 by 30 inches,
The John J. Emery Fund, 1922.104.

Late Eighteenth-Century Fashionable Accessories: In the 1780's and 1790's, luxury items like these were more likely to be imported to America than of domestic origin. *Calash Bonnet,* probably American, brown silk, gift of Benjamin Miller, 1938.10508. *Apron,* English, woven and printed silk, gift of Nellie L. Reid in memory of Harriet Fawn Reid, 1956.203. *Fan,* probably French, painted leaf and ivory sticks, gift of Mrs. J. Wayne Neff, 1894.1257. *Comb,* probably French, carved tortoise shell, gift of Mrs. William H. Taylor and Mrs. August Marx, 1934.280. *Gloves,* probably American, silk-embroidered doeskin, gift of The Estate of Margaret Clark, 1965.282. *Shoe,* probably English, embroidered silk brocade, gift of Mrs. Lucien Wulsin, 1965.384. *Angel Pendant,* Italian, ivory, gift of Renate Farmer, 1972.346. *Chatelaine,* Dutch, silver, gift of Mrs. Chase H. Davis, 1958.50.

Spencer House Doorway, woodwork and iron railings added about 1830 to the house on Sixth Street, Cincinnati, built for Oliver Spencer in 1803 and demolished in 1954, gift of The Procter and Gamble Company, 1954.502.

Adam and Eve in the Garden of Eden, printed cottons appliquéd on linen, late XVIII or early XIX century, 55 1/2 by 45 3/4 inches, bequest of Mrs. W. M. Simmons, 1965.280.

Quilt, patchwork of white and printed cottons, dated 1811, the center square printed by John Hewson, active in Philadelphia 1773-1810, died 1821, 92 by 93 inches, gift of Mary Louise Burton, 1973.400.

Portrait of William Allston by Thomas Sully, 1783-1872, oil on canvas, 1826, 29 by 24 inches, gift of Mary Kilgour Miller, Edmund Miller and Rufus King, 1918.52.

Axe Bracket in the Shape of a Fish, early XIX century, wrought iron, length 8 1/4 inches, The Carol R. Guggenheim Memorial Fund, 1958.385.

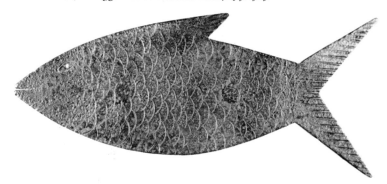

Coverlet (detail), jacquard-woven by Peter Lorentz, Wayne County, Indiana, 1837, "lilies and stars" pattern, natural cotton and red, blue and green wool, 99 by 86 inches, gift of Mrs. H. P. Rawson, 1959.57.

The Cary House Parlor, painted woodwork, marble and stone fireplace, from the house of William Cary, Hamilton Avenue, College Hill, Cincinnati, built about 1816 and demolished in 1938, gift of Mrs. Samuel Joseph, 1939.297.

The furnishings of this room and of the adjacent Bedroom, Dining Room and Hallway from the Cary House represent the kind of accumulation natural for a prosperous but careful American household in the first half of the nineteenth century, ranging in date from the late eighteenth century up to about the 1840's. The *Secretary-Bookcase* shown here, the bequest of Rose Marion Verhage, 1968.460, is of particular interest because of the rarity of pieces that can be documented as made in Cincinnati. It is signed with the stamp of William Hawkins of Fourth Street between Sycamore and Main Streets, Cincinnati, and was made in the late 1830's. The *Tall Clock,* a Museum purchase, 1966.1175, is another Cincinnati piece; it was made by Samuel Best of Cincinnati between 1802 and 1818.

View across Frenchman's Bay from Mt. Desert Island after a Squall by Thomas Cole, 1801-1848, oil on canvas, 38 1/4 by 62 1/2 inches, gift of Alice Scarborough, 1925.569.

Portrait of Thomas J. Matthews by Aaron
Haughton Corwine, 1802-1830, oil on canvas, 27
by 22 1/2 inches, bequest of Elizabeth Matthews,
1965.268.

**The Ships "Winged Arrow" and "Southern
Cross" in Boston Harbor** by Fitz Hugh Lane,
1804-1865, oil on canvas, 1853, 24 1/8 by 36 1/2
inches, The Edwin and Virginia Irwin Memorial
Fund, 1971.31.

Eve Disconsolate by Hiram Powers, 1805-1873, marble, height 76 3/16 inches, gift of Judge Nicholas Longworth, 1888.86.

Indians Hunting by John Mix Stanley, 1814-1872, oil on composition board, 10 by 8 1/8 inches, gift of The Estate of Bishop Spence Burton, 1966.642.

Order No. 11 by George Caleb Bingham, 1811-1879, oil on canvas, 55 1/2 by 78 1/2 inches, The Edwin and Virginia Irwin Memorial Fund, 1958.515.

Portrait of Andrew Jackson by Miner Kilbourne Kellogg, 1814-1889, oil on canvas, 1836, 30 1/2 by 25 1/2 inches, gift of Charles H. Kellogg, Sr., 1888.84.

Blue Hole, Flood Waters, Little Miami River by Robert S. Duncanson, about 1817-1872, oil on canvas, 1851, 29 1/4 by 42 1/4 inches, gift of Norbert Heerman, 1926.18.

Ohio Glass, 1820-1860: *Half-pint Flask,* diamond quilted, light honey amber, height 5 1/2 inches; *Cream Pitcher,* Zanesville, twenty-four ribbed, green, height 5 1/4 inches; *Grandfather Flask,* Zanesville, quart size, ribbed, golden amber, height 8 5/8 inches; *Bottle,* ribbed, light green, miniature calabash shape, height 4 3/4 inches; 1951.444, .457, .459, .462; The William T. H. Howe Collection, bequest of Edith B. Tranter.

Cincinnati Silver: *Julep Cup* by David Kinsey, active 1840-1870, gift of John S. Conner, 1910. 382. *Pitcher* by Edward Kinsey, about 1834-1860, Museum purchase, 1907.194. *Tongs* by Samuel Best, 1802-1818, Museum purchase, 1962.118.

The American Wilderness by Asher B. Durand,
1796-1865, oil on canvas, 1864, 25 1/4 by 40
inches, The Edwin and Virginia Irwin Memorial
Fund, 1968.261.

View of Kallenfels by Thomas Worthington Whittredge, 1820-1910, oil on canvas, 1856, 30 1/2 by 27 inches, gift of Mary Hanna, 1931.340

The Underground Railway by Charles T. Webber, 1825-1911, oil on canvas, 1893, 52 1/2 by 76 1/4 inches, gift by popular subscription, 1927.26.

Model for the Tyler Davidson Fountain, Cincinnati, by August von Kreling, German, 1819-1876, bronze, 1869, height 41 1/4 inches, bequest of Eugene Booth, 1952.198.

Cloister Court in the Snow by Carl Friedrich Lessing, German, 1808-1880, pencil, pen, opaque white and yellow on paper, probably about 1825, 11 1/4 by 14 1/4 inches, gift of Joseph Longworth, 1882.13.

On the Test by Sir Francis Seymour Haden, British, 1818-1910, etching and drypoint (first state), 1859, 7 3/4 by 10 1/2 inches, bequest of Herbert Greer French, 1943.721.

European Art: Late Nineteenth and Twentieth Centuries

The first Impressionist exhibition in 1874 in Paris was a turning point in the arts. In one way it was the climax of an effort dating back to the Renaissance: to reproduce the actual look of the natural world as seen by the human eye. Chemists, physicists, and physiologists all helped the painters in reaching this goal, although there were not many to cheer the winners. Manet, Sisley and Pissarro all were denounced as dangers to society. Today it is hard to understand why their gentle, pleasurable canvases once should have seemed so anarchistic.

But no sooner had Impressionism arrived and quickly spread all over the Western world than some of its originators, including Degas, Renoir and above all Cézanne, began to realize that merely seeing was not enough; the mind as well as the eye was essential to the visual experience, and the incident of sight had to be reinforced with intellectual order and analysis. Many others, such as the eccentric but brilliant Van Gogh and Toulouse-Lautrec, took part in this forward, post-Impressionist movement.

By the first years of the twentieth century a new generation began to experiment with the possibilities of an art more and more removed from the copying of observed nature. Redon turned inward to plumb the unconscious mind, and a generation of Surrealists followed him. The Intimistes Bonnard and Vuillard went their quiet way. Far more immediately exciting were the Fauves, or "wild beasts," who took their title from a critic's remark and who explored a new world of vivid color and bold design under the leadership of Matisse, Derain and Rouault.

Contemporary with the Fauves, and possibly more influential, were the mathematically-minded Cubists, who took their appropriate name from a slighting comment by Matisse. Picasso and Braque were the inventors of Cubism, though the versatile genius of Picasso cannot be confined to any one category. There were many enthusiastic disciples, Juan Gris and Léger among them. Almost the whole of abstract, ultimately non-objective art derives from them.

The "School of Paris" is the encompassing name given to all these apparently new departures, the magnetic forces that drew Modigliani, Chagall, Miró, Arp, Lipchitz and many others to the French capital from abroad, followed by the younger deStaël and Vieira daSilva. Its powerful influences affected the equally colorful developments taking place in middle Europe, the Lowlands and Scandinavia, even in Russia for a short time in the early 'twenties. Klee, Kandinsky, and Nolde all reflect these currents.

Architecture and design were not far behind the painters and sculptors, sometimes even ahead of them. Nineteenth-century European decorative arts, bombarded by technological advances with which they constantly were experimenting, in retrospect seem not to have achieved one overall identifying style comparable to preceding periods. By the twentieth century, however, the machine with its capacities for artistic expression has come under the disciplined control of designers and craftsmen who put it to effective modern use.

Cabbage Patch near the Village by Camille Pissarro, French, 1830-1903, oil on canvas, 1875, 21 1/4 by 25 1/2 inches, gift of Albert P. Strietmann, 1952.240.

Women at the Races by Edouard Manet, French, 1832-1883, oil on canvas, 1865, 16 5/8 by 12 5/8 inches, The Fanny Bryce Lehmer Fund, 1944.105.

Two Nude Men by Hilaire Germain Edgar Degas, French, 1834-1917, pencil on gray paper, 1856, 10 by 8 1/4 inches, possibly a study for *Dante and Vergil*, Museum purchase, 1920.41.

Dancer in Her Dressing Room by Hilaire Germain Edgar Degas, French, 1834-1917, pastel on paper, about 1879, 34 5/8 by 14 7/8 inches, bequest of Mary Hanna, 1956.114.

Still Life with Bread and Eggs by Paul Cézanne,
French, 1839-1906, oil on canvas, 1865, 23 1/4 by
30 inches, anonymous gift, 1955.73.

Self-Portrait and Apple by Paul Cézanne, French 1839-1906, pencil on paper, 6 3/4 by 9 inches, gift of Emily Poole, 1958.128.

The River at the Bridge of Les Trois Sautets by Paul Cézanne, French, 1839-1906, watercolor on paper, 16 by 21 inches, gift of John J. Emery, 1951.298.

The Evil Spirits by Auguste Rodin, French, 1840-1917, bronze, 1886, height 12 13/16 inches, gift of John B. Hollister, 1958.476.

Return of the Prodigal Son by Jean-Louis Forain, French, 1852-1931, etching, 11 11/16 by 17 3/8 inches, Mr. and Mrs. Ross W. Sloniker Collection of Twentieth Century Biblical and Religious Prints, 1953.297.

Mlle. Jeanne Samary by Pierre Auguste Renoir, French, 1841-1919, pastel on paper, about 1877, 26 1/2 by 18 1/4 inches, gift of Mary Hanna, 1946.107.

Undergrowth with Two Figures by Vincent van
Gogh, Dutch, 1853-1890, oil on canvas, 1890,
19 1/2 by 39 1/4 inches, bequest of Mary E.
Johnston, 1967.1430.

Chestnut Trees by Lovis Corinth, German, 1858-
1923, drypoint, 1923, 9 1/2 by 10 7/8 inches,
The Albert P. Strietmann Collection, 1968.526.

At the Concert by Henri de Toulouse-Lautrec, French, 1864-1901, color lithograph poster (third state), 1896, for the Ault & Wiborg Co., Cincinnati, 14 1/2 by 10 3/8 inches, The Albert P. Strietmann Collection, 1964.187.

Small Worlds III by Vassily Kandinsky, Russian, 1866-1944, color lithograph, 1922, 11 by 9 inches, The Albert P. Strietmann Collection, 1965.489.

La Revue Blanche by Pierre Bonnard, French,
1867-1940, color lithograph poster, 1894, 30 1/8
by 23 inches, gift of Albert P. Strietmann,
1959.157.

The Three Kings by Emil Nolde, German, 1867-
1956, color lithograph, 1913, 25 1/4 by 21 inches,
Mr. and Mrs. Ross W. Sloniker Collection of
Twentieth Century Biblical and Religious Prints,
1955.445.

Rumanian Blouse by Henri Matisse, French,
1869-1954, oil on canvas, 1937, 28 3/4 by 23 5/8
inches, bequest of Mary E. Johnston, 1967.1427.

The Tuileries Garden by Jean-Edouard Vuillard,
French, 1867-1940, from *L'album des peintres-
graveurs*, color lithograph, 1896, 13 7/8 by 18
inches, gift of Albert P. Strietmann, 1954.179.

Nocturne by Georges Rouault, French, 1871-1958, oil on cardboard, 1939, 28 1/4 by 39 1/4 inches, bequest of Mary E. Johnston, 1967.1121.

Outdoor Theater by Paul Klee, Swiss, 1879-1940, watercolor on paper, 1914, 9 1/4 by 11 7/8 inches, bequest of Mary E. Johnston, 1967.1319.

Goatherd by Ernst Ludwig Kirchner, German, 1880-1938, woodcut (third state), 1918, 18 13/16 by 15 1/16 inches, The Albert P. Strietmann Collection, 1964.114.

The Three Baskets by André Derain, French, 1880-1954, oil on canvas, 1937, 54 by 54 1/4 inches, gift of John W. Warrington in memory of his mother, Elsie Holmes Warrington, 1941.6.

Head of a Woman by Pablo Picasso, Spanish, 1881-1973, oil on canvas, 1922, 24 3/32 by 19 11/16 inches, The Fanny Bryce Lehmer Fund, 1941.253.

Compote, Bread and Cheese by Georges Braque, French, 1882-1963, oil and sand on canvas, 1941, 14 1/8 by 47 1/4 inches, bequest of Mary E. Johnston, 1967.1317.

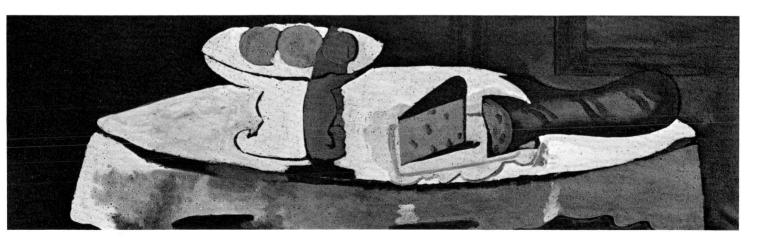

Still Life with Glasses by Georges Braque, French, 1882-1963, etching, 1912 (1950 edition), 13 5/8 by 8 1/4 inches, gift of Albert P. Strietmann, 1955.756.

Portrait of Max Jacob by Amedeo Modigliani, Italian, 1884-1920, oil on canvas, about 1916, 36 1/2 by 23 3/4 inches, gift of Mary E. Johnston, 1959.43.

Still Life with Violin and Music Sheet by Juan Gris (José Victoriano Gonzalez), Spanish, 1887-1927, oil and collage on canvas, 1913, 36 1/2 by 26 inches, bequest of Mary E. Johnston, 1967.1112.

The Red Rooster by Marc Chagall, French (born in Russia), 1887- , oil on canvas, 1940, 28 3/4 by 36 inches, bequest of Mary E. Johnston, 1967.1426.

Wheel by Jean (Hans) Arp, French, 1888-1966,
oil on paper, 1930, 41 1/4 by 29 5/8 inches,
bequest of Mary E. Johnston, 1967.1104.

Mountain by Rolf Nesch, Norwegian (born in
Germany), 1893- , from the series *Schnee,* collage
metal print and drypoint, 1933-34, 22 11/16 by
16 15/16 inches, gift of The Cincinnati Print and
Drawing Circle, 1959.83.

Day and Night by Maurits Cornelis Escher, Dutch, 1898-1972, color woodcut, 1938, 15 3/8 by 26 5/8 inches, gift of The Museum Shop Committee and Volunteers, 1973.496.

Fern in the Hat by Jean Dubuffet, French, 1901- , color lithograph, 1953, 20 1/2 by 15 1/2 inches, Museum purchase, 1955.643.

The Port of Dunkerque by Nicolas de Staël,
French (born in Russia), 1914-1955, oil on
canvas, 1954, 23 5/8 by 32 inches, bequest of
Mary E. Johnston, 1967.1107.

Flanders by Maria-Helena Vieira da Silva, Portuguese, 1908- , oil on canvas, 1960, 57 7/8 by 64 1/8 inches, bequest of Mary E. Johnston, 1967.1125.

The Groesbeck Parlor, gilded wood cornices and frames, mirrors, interior shutters and chandelier from Elmhurst, the house of William Slocum Groesbeck, on the present Elmhurst Place, Cincinnati, built 1871-72, demolished in 1941, gift of Mrs. Daniel Riker and Mrs. Hartwell Cabot, 1941.227.

This room, furnished in the style now called Victorian, but called Modern in its day, reflects the taste of the rich merchants of the post-Civil War period. The suite of laminated and carved *Chairs, Sofa* and *Table* ordered from John Belter, New York, in 1863 by Mr. and Mrs. Julius Freiberg of Cincinnati, was given to the Museum by Mr. and Mrs. Albert M. Freiberg, 1959.53-56. The monumental Sèvres *Urns* and supporting ebonized wood and ormolu *Cabinets* were imported from France for the Reakirt mansion in Cincinnati and bequeathed to the Museum by Llewellyn B. Reakirt, 1949.74-75. The figures wear the equally elaborate and costly apparel of the 1870's to 1890's.

Falls of the Tequendama near Bogota, New Granada, by Frederic E. Church, 1826-1900, oil on canvas, 1854, 64 by 40 inches, The Edwin and Virginia Irwin Memorial Fund, 1971.30.

American Art: Late Nineteenth and Twentieth Centuries

The history of American and European arts over the past two centuries has been so interrelated and cross-fertilized that to make a division between them is necessarily arbitrary. Most American artists until the twentieth century were only a generation or two removed from European forebears, or were products of European training or worked on both sides of the Atlantic. And wealthy Americans imported works by European artists of their day. Joseph Longworth of Cincinnati bought more than 800 drawings by Carl Friedrich Lessing of Düsseldorf, which he gave to the Museum in 1882, and the model for Cincinnati's civic symbol, the locally famous Tyler Davidson Fountain, was commissioned in the 1870's from August von Kreling of Munich.

Düsseldorf and Munich were popular training fields for many American artists of the second half of the nineteenth century, and Cincinnati's Frank Duveneck was perhaps the most important product, German or American, of the Munich Academy. He not only taught in Munich and Italy, but returned to transmit the primarily Germanic principles to generations of American students, some of them major names in American painting.

Before long, however, Paris became the ultimate haven for Americans as well as Europeans. Almost everyone was affected, directly or indirectly. George Inness and even Winslow Homer felt their styles and concepts broaden in the air of Paris, and some like John Henry Twachtman brought home the pure seeds of Impressionism to naturalize them in American soil. These men were rather more than American artists; they were artists by any definition who happened to be American.

Certainly this was true of such international figures as James Abbott McNeill Whistler and John Singer Sargent, and of Mary Cassatt of Pennsylvania, considered one of the foremost French Impressionists.

Sargent's influence is clearly seen in Robert Blum, while Albert Pinkham Ryder is one of the true originals, poet and mystic almost in the pattern of Blake, but a far stronger painter. Alsatian-born Henry François Farny continued the tradition of western subject matter, but set his Indians in a most natural and unromanticized western landscape. The sculptor Augustus Saint-Gaudens, also of French descent, created the model for the best of official American monumental sculpture; New York-born Jacob Epstein, on the other hand, developed his distinctive post-Rodin sculpture style in London, to be rewarded with a knighthood.

The Armory Show of 1913 suddenly confronted American artists with the challenge of European modernism. It was both a shock and a stimulus, from which a few strong figures emerged: Marsden Hartley, Charles Sheeler, Edward Hopper and especially Walt Kuhn who had been largely responsible for the Show. A self-conscious American regionalism and art of social protest dominated the 'thirties, with only Grant Wood in at least two of his best-known paintings surviving as a major figure.

Hans Hofmann emigrated from Germany in 1930 to become one of the most effective teachers in the country, and toward the end of his life one of America's most distinguished painters. Alexander Calder is the third in the line of a family of American sculptors and continues to enrich the international scene with his innovative, often witty mobile and stabile sculptures. He was one of the new American artists to turn European eyes westward with an at first grudging but now growing respect.

In the long list of established twentieth century artists are the sculptors David Smith and Wilfred Zogbaum who died untimely with much accomplished. Prominent also are Richard Diebenkorn of California, Helen Frankenthaler of New York, and Jim Dine, Tom Wesselmann and R. B. Kitaj of Ohio, as well as the sculptor-printmaker Louise Nevelson, and the painter-printmakers Jasper Johns and Willem De Kooning.

As this century enters its final quarter there are many indications that the center of artistic vitality is shifting from the Old World to the New. Although European influences continue to be felt, it is to American art that critical attention turns for keys to future artistic directions in the established mediums as well as in the many experimental, still-emerging modes of creative expression.

The Last Arrow by Randolph Rogers, 1825-1892, bronze, about 1879-80, height 43 3/4 inches, gift of O. J. Wilson, 1888.293.

Fashions of the 1880's: *Dress* by Worth, Paris, black brocaded satin and pink satin, gift of Mrs. Johnson McGuire and Mrs. Virginius Hall, 1971.152. *Dress,* gray-blue, striped pile silk and rust silk twill, gift of Isabelle and Margaret Fisk, 1972.247.

Near the Village, October, by George Inness, 1825-1894, oil on canvas, 1892, 30 by 45 inches, gift of Emilie L. Heine in memory of Mr. and Mrs. John Hauck, 1940.943.

Arrangement in Pink and Purple by James Abbott
McNeill Whistler, 1834-1903, oil on wood, 12
by 9 inches, The John J. Emery Fund, 1920.38.

Rotherhithe by James Abbott McNeill Whistler,
1834-1903, from *Sixteen Etchings of Scenes on
the Thames,* etching (third state), 1860, 10 7/8
by 7 7/8 inches, bequest of Herbert Greer French,
1943.588.

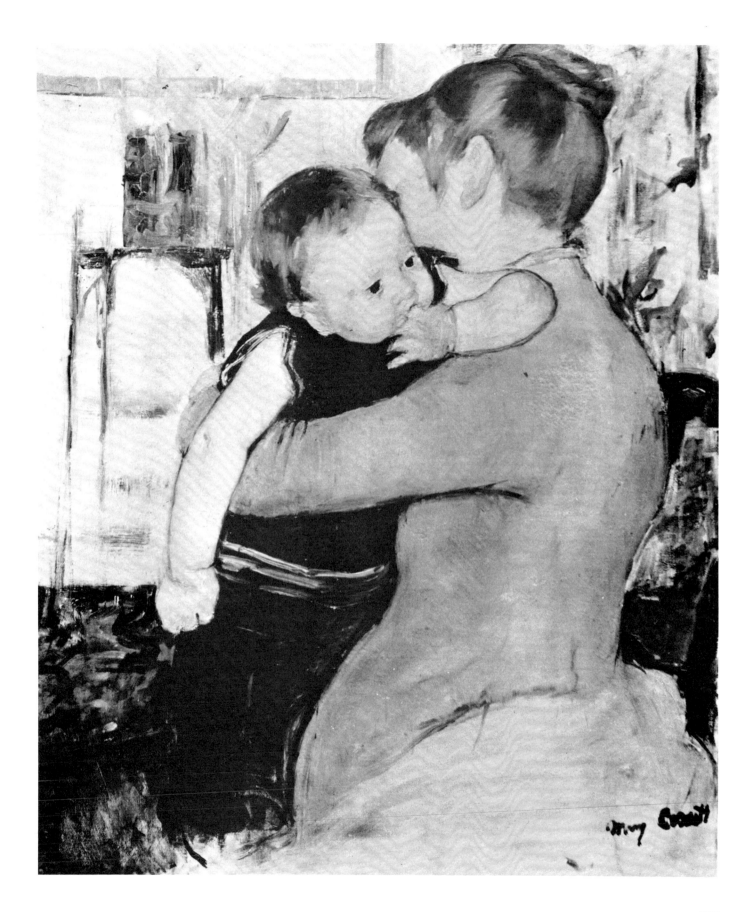

Autumn's Golden Pathway by Albert Pinkham
Ryder, 1847-1917, oil on wood. 1914, 8 11/16 by
5 15/16 inches, The Edwin and Virginia Irwin
Memorial Fund, 1966.268.

Stanley Matthews and His Wife, Mary, by
Augustus Saint-Gaudens, 1848-1907, bronze,
1904, 32 5/8 by 47 inches, gift of T. S. Matthews,
1955.795.

Whistling Boy by Frank Duveneck, 1848-1919,
oil on canvas, 1872, 28 by 21 1/2 inches, gift of
the artist, 1904.196.

Portrait of Elizabeth Boott Duveneck by Frank
Duveneck, 1848-1919, oil on canvas, 1888, 65 3/8
by 34 3/4 inches, gift of the artist, 1915.78.

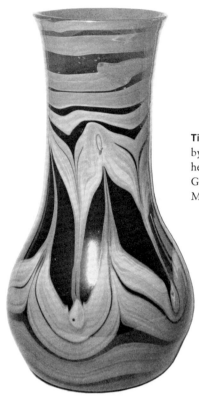

Tiffany Favrile Glass Vase, about 1897, designed by Louis Comfort Tiffany, New York, 1848-1933, height 16 1/8 inches, gift of Alfred Traber Goshorn, first Director of the Cincinnati Art Museum, 1897.122.

Fashions of the Turn of the Century: *Coat,* American, Venise tape lace over silk, 1900-1910, gift of Ralph E. Clark, Jr., 1966.1223; *Cape* American, embroidered wool broadcloth imported from eastern Europe or Turkey, 1890's, gift of Dorothy Conway Rush, 1973.535; *Dress* by Worth, Paris, silk brocade, silk velvet, beaded flower trim, silk fringe and lace, 1895, gift of Frederick and Tecla T. Haldy, 1926.174.

Bookcase-Secretary by Benn Pitman and his wife and daughters, Cincinnati, carved wood, about 1884, height 60 1/4 inches, gift of Melrose Pitman, 1969.387.

Old Holley House, Cos Cob, by John H. Twachtman, 1853-1902, oil on canvas, about 1890-1900, 25 by 25 inches, The John J. Emery Fund, 1916.3.

Italian Girl with Fan by John Singer Sargent, 1856-1925, oil on canvas, 1882-83, 93 3/4 by 52 1/2 inches, The Edwin and Virginia Irwin Memorial Fund, 1972.37.

Venetian Lace Makers by Robert Frederick Blum, 1857-1903, oil on canvas, 1887, 30 by 41 inches, gift of Elizabeth S. Potter, 1905.8.

Ewer by Kataro Shirayamadani 1865-1948, Rookwood pottery with Gorham silver overlay, 1890, height 9 3/8 inches, Museum purchase, 1973.104.

"Skyscraper" Bookcase by Paul Theodore Frankl, 1876-1962, California redwood with base band of nickel-plated steel, 1920's, height 90 inches, gift of the Estate of Mrs. James M. Hutton II through James M. Hutton III, 1969.418.

Woolworth Building by John Marin, 1870-1953, etching (second state) 1913, 12 7/8 by 11 7/16 inches, The Albert P. Strietmann Collection, 1960.783.

Dress, about 1927, satin, silk fringe and silver beads, gift of Mrs. Eugene W. Kettering, 1973.164.

Tricorne by Walt Kuhn, 1877-1949, oil on canvas, 1939, 27 1/8 by 21 1/4 inches, The Edwin and Virginia Irwin Memorial Fund, 1957.148.

Valley Road by Marsden Hartley, 1878-1943, oil on canvas, about 1919-20, 24 by 28 inches, The Edwin and Virginia Irwin Memorial Fund, 1968.47.

Toward Crepuscule by Hans Hofmann, 1880-1966, oil on canvas, 1963, 60 by 72 inches, The Edwin and Virginia Irwin Memorial Fund, 1968.264.

Portrait of Rabindranath Tagore by Sir Jacob Epstein, 1880-1959, bronze, 1926, height 19 5/16 inches, gift of Mr. and Mrs. Leonard R. Minster, 1966.39.

Street Scene, Gloucester, by Edward Hopper, 1882-1967, oil on canvas, 28 by 36 1/4 inches, The Edwin and Virginia Irwin Memorial Fund, 1959.49.

The Upstairs by Charles Sheeler, 1883-1965, oil on canvas, 1938, 19 1/2 by 12 3/4 inches, The Fanny Bryce Lehmer Fund, 1938.10557.

Pegasus by Jacques Lipchitz (born in Lithuania), 1891-1973, bronze, 1944, height 15 1/2 inches, gift of The Cincinnati Modern Art Society, 1951.189.

Daughters of Revolution by Grant Wood, 1892-1942, oil on masonite, 1932, 20 by 40 inches, The Edwin and Virginia Irwin Memorial Fund, 1959.46.

Twenty Leaves and an Apple by Alexander
Calder, 1898- , painted sheet metal and piano
wire, 1946, height about 48 inches, gift of
Thomas Emery's Sons, Inc. 1965-516.

Untitled from the series *Aquatints* by Louise
Nevelson (born in Russia), 1900- , aquatint and
foil collage, 1973, 27 15/16 by 21 9/16 inches,
gift of her friends in memory of Emily Poole,
1973.621.

Entrance by David Smith, 1906-1965, steel, 1951, height 31 13/16 inches, gift of The Cincinnati Modern Art Society, 1954.176.

Spacial Movement by Dominick Labino, 1910- , Grand Rapids, Ohio, silver-copper opalescent glass, December 1970, height 7 1/8 inches, The Jane Thomson Herschede Memorial Fund, 1971.253.

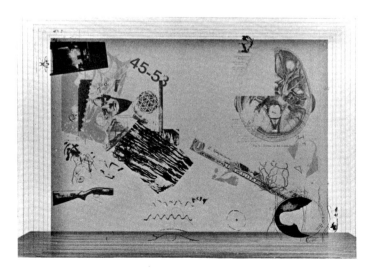

Plexigram VIII by John Cage, 1912- , and Calvin J. Sumsion, 1942- , from the series *Not Wanting to Say Anything About Marcel,* color screen print on eight plexiglas sheets, 1968-73, 14 1/4 by 20 by 14 1/2 inches, The Albert P. Strietmann Collection, 1972.517.

Great Captain Rocks by Wilfred Zogbaum,
1915-1965, painted steel and stone, 1960, height
59 inches, Museum purchase, 1968.524.

Interior with View of Buildings by Richard
Diebenkorn, 1922- , oil on canvas, 1962, 84 by
67 inches, The Edwin and Virginia Irwin
Memorial Fund, 1964.68.

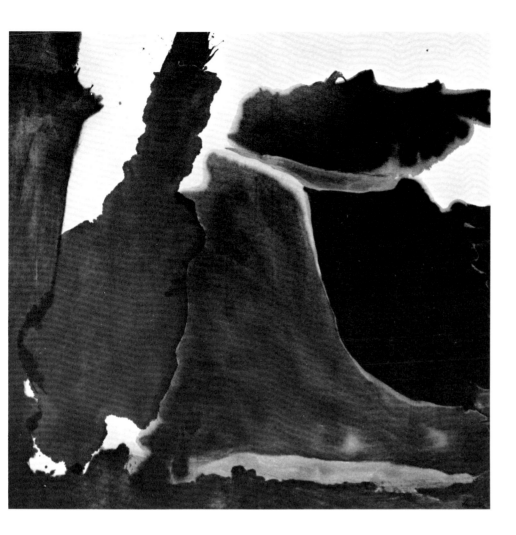

Rock Pond by Helen Frankenthaler, 1928- ,
acrylic on canvas, 1962-63, 80 by 82 inches, The
Edwin and Virginia Irwin Memorial Fund,
1969.11.

Dress by Geoffrey Beene, printed silk chiffon,
1964, gift of Geoffrey Beene, 1966.184.

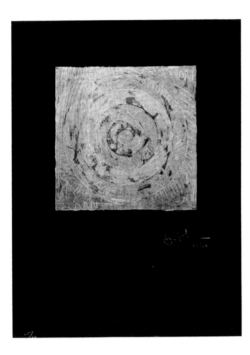

White Target by Jasper Johns, 1930- , color lithograph, 1967-68, 13 by 13 inches, The Albert P. Strietmann Collection, 1969.581.

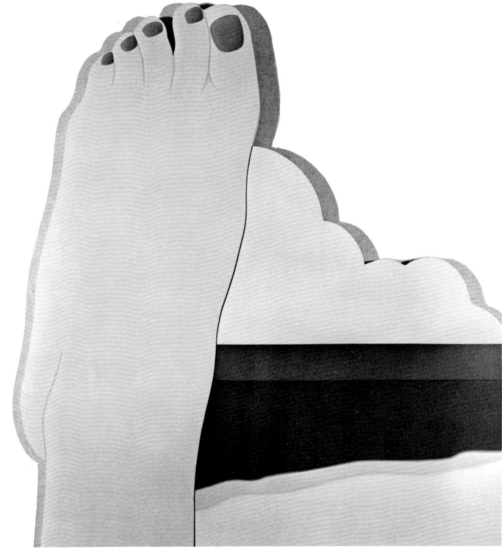

Seascape #21 by Tom Wesselmann, 1931- , oil on canvas, 1967, 108 by 96 inches, gift of the artist, 1969.842.

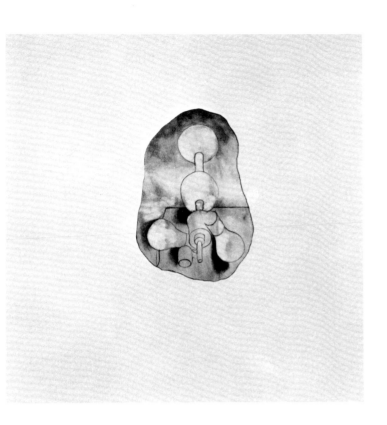

Light over My Bed Coming through Nassau Pink
by Jim Dine, 1935- , oil on canvas, 1965, 60 by 60 inches, The Edwin and Virginia Irwin Memorial Fund, 1966.32.

Apotheosis of Groundlessness by Ronald B. Kitaj, 1932- , oil on canvas, 1964, 60 by 84 inches The Edwin and Virginia Irwin Memorial Fund, 1968.265.

Woman Holding Calabash Rattles, probably from the Ashira-Bapunu tribes of the Ogowe River area north of the mouth of the Congo, collected before 1890, wood with inlaid glass eyes, applied string and wire, height 16 5/8 inches, gift by subscription, 1890.1545.

Mask, probably from the Ogowe River area, collected before 1890, painted wood, height 9 15/16 inches, gift by subscription, 1890.849.

Weight for Gold Dust in the Form of a Scorpion, Ashanti, XIX century, brass, height 1 1/16 inches, gift of Raymond Wielgus through Julius Carlebach, 1956.210.

African Art

The era of exploration and the rise of colonial empires disclosed many hitherto unknown peoples and their cultures. The growing sciences of ethnology and anthropology studied them earnestly and profitably, but it was not until the opening years of the twentieth century that experimental modern artists discovered almost simultaneously, in the natural history museums of Dresden and Paris, guild brothers among the artist-craftsmen of Africa, Polynesia and the Americas.

The work of the latter is sometimes called "primitive," but this is a misnomer, signifying as it does the beginning phases, sometimes crude and fumbling, of later mature accomplishments. Certainly it does not apply to the sophisticated form sense of West African sculpture. The word also has more than a tinge of condescension, implying that these fine arts are inferior simply because they are not in the main stream of Graeco-Roman classicism reinforced by the teaching of the Renaissance and later Academies. Rebels against that tradition found in the so-called "primitive art" a new vein of artistic ideas to be enthusiastically mined.

The examples of these exotic cultures shown in the Museum have been selected for their artistry from the Museum's large ethnological collection which was formed in days when anything rare, curious or informative was considered suitable to an art museum. The masks, chief's staff, votive figures and other objects intended for ritual use project the enormous vitality of the spiritual purposes they served, but the same intensity of observation and inventiveness is lavished on objects like the weights used in trade for measuring gold dust and on other objects of everyday utility.

Fetish: Standing Man, probably from the Basonga tribe, wood, height 9 3/8 inches, gift of Raymond Wielgus through Julius Carlebach, 1956.213.

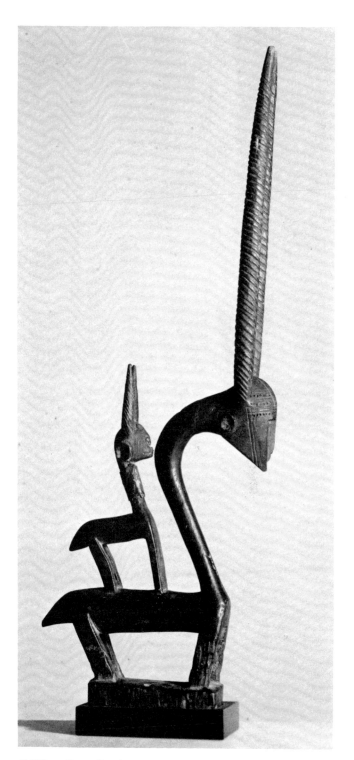

Chi Wara, Dance Headpiece: Antelope and Young, Bambara tribe, Mali, wood, height 26 3/8 inches, gift of Mary Mills Ford, Olive Lloyd Mills and Marcia Mills Bogert in memory of Edward Lloyd Mills, 1964.157.

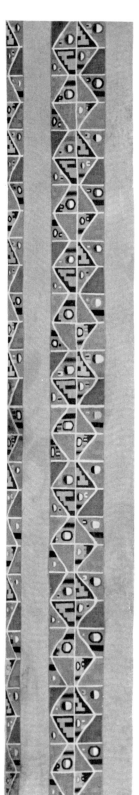

Panel from a Shirt, Peruvian, Huari or Tiahuanaco period, about 600-1100 A. D., woven dyed wool, 83 1/16 by 14 1/8 inches, gift of Mr. and Mrs. John Becker, 1972.465.

Seated-Warrior Vessel, Peruvian, Mochica period, about 400-1000 A. D., painted pottery, height 9 1/4 inches, gift of F. Schultz through The Women's Art Museum Association, 1881.215.

Face-Collar Jar, Peruvian, Tiahuanaco period, about 1000-1300 A D., painted pottery, height 9 1/4 inches, gift of Mr. and Mrs. Julius Fleischmann, 1938.10590.

South America

American Indian Art

The American Indians are believed to have migrated from Asia to the Western Hemisphere some 10,000 years or more before Christ, bringing with them only the simplest of chipped stone tools. Although it is possible that some technological advances may have reached them from Asia at later dates, it appears that they discovered for themselves basket and textile weaving, pottery, agriculture and, eventually, architecture, sculpture and painting.

The tribal divisions of the early Americas were as numerous as those of early Europe or Asia, and each tribe developed its own patterns for useful and ritual objects.

The Pre-Columbian pottery and textiles recovered from Peruvian burials exhibit not only great skill but a sophisticated sense of form and color and sometimes a wry sense of humor. Different motifs, but an equally high degree of design sense, appear on the pottery of the semi-desert areas of southwestern United States and northern Mexico, developed long before the arrival of Europeans and continuing down to the present day. Marine and forest creatures—whales, walrus, waterfowl, beavers, bears—characterize the art of the Northwest Coast which is enhanced by the use of bright colors, mother of pearl and walrus ivory. In the Great Plains, hides worked into garments, tents and bags were decorated with paint, dyed porcupine quills, shells, feathers and, after the Europeans arrived, beads, silk, dyed cloth and pieces of metal.

The prehistoric inhabitants of the Ohio-Mississippi river basin built mounds in the shapes of serpents, birds and other creatures and, finally, great earthen pyramids. These Moundbuilders left burial offerings of pottery, ranging from crude to very sophisticated, ceremonial objects of chipped, ground and polished stone, fresh-water pearls, engraved shells, copper, mica, obsidian and other materials traded over long distances.

Although the beliefs and traditions embodied in these works of art may never be fully comprehended, their visual impact is immediate and universally appealing.

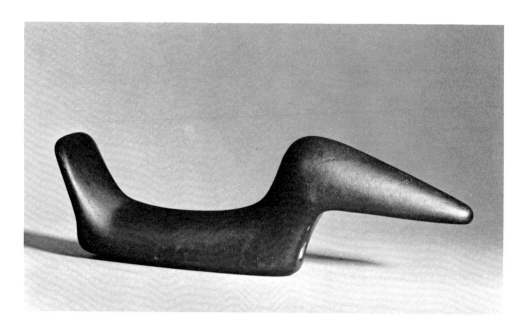

Bird Stone, Ohio Valley, late Archaic or early Woodland culture, about 2000-1000 B. C., ground and polished stone, height 2 inches, found in the vicinity of Cincinnati, Ohio, before 1888, gift of the Honorable Joseph Cox, 1888.512.

The Waverly Tablet, Ohio Valley, Adena culture, about 300 B. C., ground and engraved shale, height 3 3/8 inches, found 1885 in a mound on the property of Abraham Cutlip between Waverly and Piketon, Ohio, gift of Mrs. William M. Galt, 1939.140.

North America

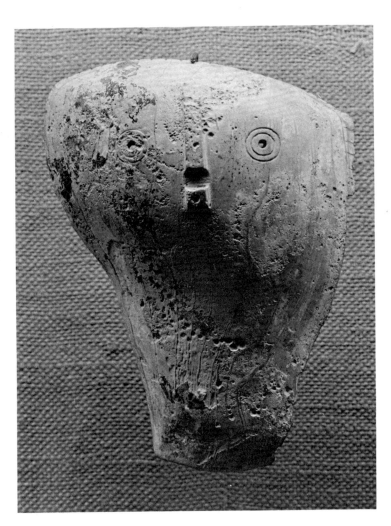

Mask, probably from a mound in Tennessee, Mississippian culture, Temple Mound I period, about 800 A. D., carved shell, height 7 15/16 inches, gift of Thomas Cleneay, 1887.20607.

Mask, late Mississippian culture, Temple Mound II period, about 1200 A. D., ground stone, height 8 1/2 inches, 1938.5124.

Stone masks are uncommon in North America but have occasionally been found in Tennessee and adjacent states in a context roughly contemporary with the final expansion of the great Temple Mound at Cahokia, Illinois. A few have also been found in northern Kentucky and southern Ohio, probably having been traded there soon after they were made.

Pedestal Bowl, from Madisonville, Ohio, Fort Ancient culture, 1350-1650 A. D., pottery, height 7 3/4 inches, gift of the Honorable Joseph Cox, 1888.715.

Pitcher, from Chaco Canyon, New Mexico, probably Pueblo II period, about 900-1100 A. D., painted pottery, height 6 1/2 inches, gift of Amelia Elizabeth White, 1937.531.

Bowl, from Mimbres Valley, New Mexico, Mogollon V period, about 1100-1400 A. D., painted pottery, diameter 8 1/4 inches, gift of Mrs. Owen, 1901.48.

Bowl, Zuni, New Mexico, XIX century A. D., painted pottery, height 11 1/2 inches, gift of the Women's Art Museum Association, 1885.48.

Effigy Bowl, from Casas Grandes, northern Mexico, Late period, after about 1300 A. D., painted pottery, height 7 1/2 inches, Museum purchase, 1929.227.

Water Jar, from Acoma pueblo, New Mexico, XIX century A. D., painted pottery, height 8 3/4 inches, gift of W. N. King, 1906.61.

Porcupine-Quill Embroidery on Buckskin, from the Great Plains, XIX-XX century A. D.: *Knife Sheath, Legging-Moccasins*, Sioux, gift of Nettleton Neff, 1891.2954-2955. *Medicine Pouch*, Shawnee, gift of Annie and Catherine James, 1927.471. *Cuffs*, gift of Amelia Elizabeth White, 1937.550.

Baskets, from California, XIX century A. D., Pomo, Yokut and Karok tribes, coiled and twined vegetable fibers, and shell, bead and feather applications, from left to right: gift of Amelia Elizabeth White, 1937.507; gift of W. N. King, 1906.146; bequest of Eleanor I. Earnshaw, 1912.362, 1912.354.

Totem Pole, Haida tribe, Northwest Coast of North America, XIX century A. D., argillite, height 11 1/8 inches, bequest of Charlotte H. Mackenzie, 1936.556.

Rattle, Haida tribe, Northwest Coast of North America, XIX century A. D., painted wood, length 13 inches, gift of William Howard Doane, 1914.76.

Mask, Chilkat tribe, Alaska, XIX century A.D., painted wood, applied hair and teeth, height 6 inches, gift of Dr. and Mrs. W. W. Seely, 1889.294.

Mask, Chilkat tribe, Alaska, XIX century A. D., painted wood, height 7 inches, gift of Dr. and Mrs. W. W. Seely, 1889.292.

Vessel with Duck's Head, Tlingit tribe, Northwest Coast of North America, XIX century A. D., mountain-sheep horn, height 4 7/8 inches, X-1965.15.

First Floor

Galleries

2-7: Arts of Ancient Civilizations (Egypt, Greece and Rome)

8-12: Arts of Late Roman Empire and Medieval Europe

13, 14: Musical Instruments

15-42: European and American Decorative Arts, Period Rooms, Costumes and Textiles

43-56: Arts of Ancient and Islamic Near East

57-63: Arts of the Far East

CR: Coatroom

TL: Public Telephone

M: Men's Rest Room

W: Women's Rest Room

EL: Elevator

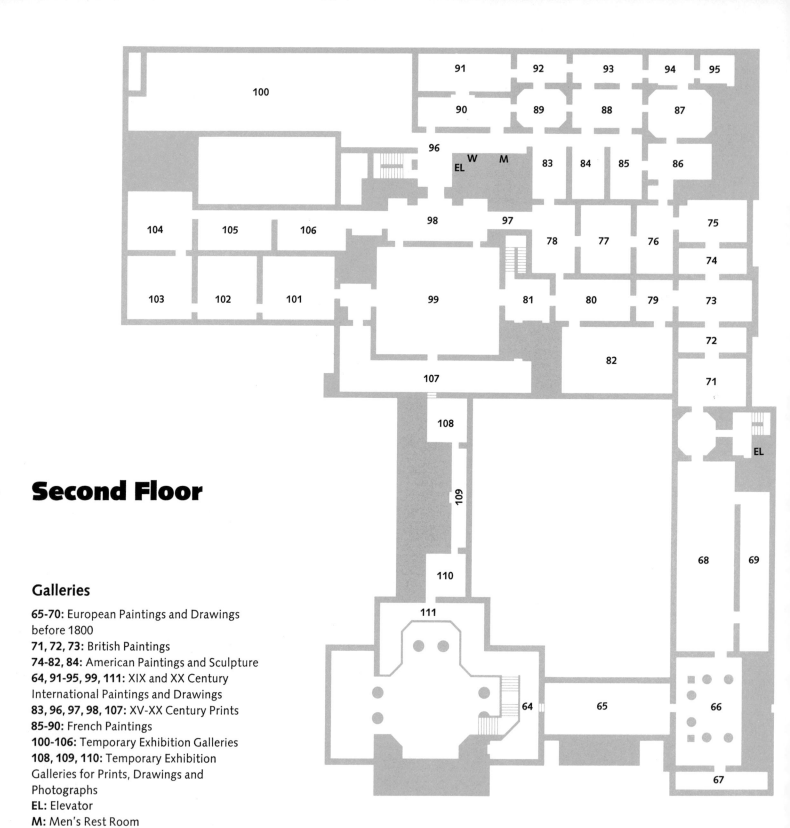

Second Floor

Galleries

65-70: European Paintings and Drawings before 1800
71, 72, 73: British Paintings
74-82, 84: American Paintings and Sculpture
64, 91-95, 99, 111: XIX and XX Century International Paintings and Drawings
83, 96, 97, 98, 107: XV-XX Century Prints
85-90: French Paintings
100-106: Temporary Exhibition Galleries
108, 109, 110: Temporary Exhibition Galleries for Prints, Drawings and Photographs
EL: Elevator
M: Men's Rest Room
W: Women's Rest Room

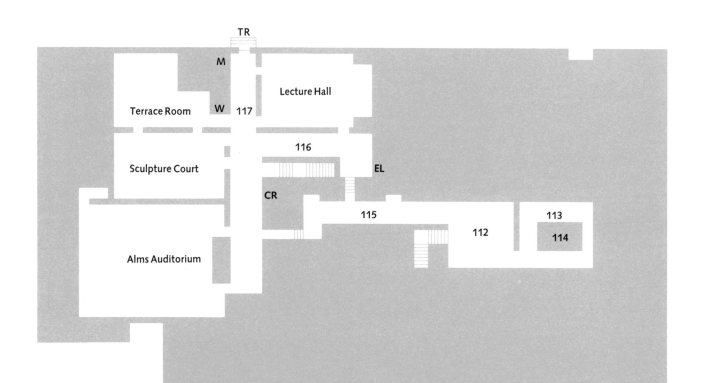

Ground Floor

Galleries

112-115: Arts of Near and Far East
116, 117: American Paintings
TR: Terrace Room Door (entrance door for most special events after 5 p.m.)
EW: Emery Wing Door (entrance for handicapped, by appointment)
CR: Coatroom
M: Men's Rest Room
W: Women's Rest Room
EL: Elevator

Museum Cafeteria Public Hours:
Monday-Friday, 12:30-3:30 p.m.,
Saturday, 11:30 a.m.-2:30 p.m.
Closed Sundays, Holidays.
(Groups of 10-30 by appointment in advance, through Public Service Office.)